CW01496970

Adoption and Loss

The Hidden Grief

21st CENTURY EDITION

Evelyn Robinson, OAM

Adoption and Loss

First published in Australia in 2000
Revised edition published in 2003
Reprinted in 2005

This edition published in 2018 by

Clova Publications
PO Box 328
Christies Beach
South Australia
Australia 5165

For further information on the author and her work, visit:
www.clovapublications.com

ISBN: 978-1729816882

By the same author:

Adoption and Recovery – *Solving the mystery of reunion*
ISBN: 978-1729855379
Published in Australia by
Clova Publications in 2004
Reprinted in 2018

In her second book, **Adoption and Recovery – Solving the mystery of reunion***, Evelyn moves on from exploring the losses associated with adoption separation, which she described so movingly and accurately in her first book and sheds much-needed light on the path to recovery for family members separated by adoption. Evelyn Robinson was the first author ever to explain the adoption reunion experience within a framework of grief resolution. In this pioneering work, Evelyn has illustrated her theory of adoption loss and recovery by including a selection of the questions which have been raised throughout her many years of experience in the world of post-adoption counselling and support. Readers will find her answers both insightful and practical.*

Adoption Reunion – *Ecstasy or Agony?*
ISBN: 978-1729855393
Published in Australia by
Clova Publications in 2009
Reprinted in 2018

In Evelyn's third book, **Adoption Reunion – Ecstasy or Agony?***, she has summarised much of the information in her first two books and added some new material. It is an ideal pocket-sized book for the reader who wants a practical, straightforward explanation of the dynamics of adoption separation and reunion, written in an accessible style. It includes some of the questions published in* **Adoption and Recovery** *as well as many new questions and answers never before published.*

Adoption and Loss

Adoption Separation – *Then and now*

ISBN: 978-1729855348
Published in Australia by
Clova Publications in 2010
Reprinted in 2018

*Since the publication of **Adoption and Loss** – **The Hidden Grief** in 2000, many parents around the world, who had been separated from their children by adoption in the twentieth century, have made contact with Evelyn.* **Adoption Separation** – **Then and now** *is a collection of their personal accounts. Evelyn received contributions from Australia, Canada, England, Ireland, New Zealand, Scotland and the United States and was struck by the similarities in their experiences, as well as their uniqueness. This is the first book to bring together the experiences of adoption separation of mothers and fathers around the world and has been very successful in illustrating the pressures faced by those who had created a child at a time and under circumstances which caused them to be alienated from their communities and ultimately to be separated from those children by adoption. By way of contrast, Evelyn has included a small selection of articles which she has written in the twenty-first century, addressing some current issues in relation to adoption, such as the pivotal first government apology for past adoptions, which Evelyn attended with her son, Stephen, in Western Australia in 2010.*

———————————————

This book is dedicated to my dear Mother, who showed more generosity of spirit in her life than anyone I ever knew.

The Hidden Grief

Adoption and Loss – *The Hidden Grief*

*Evelyn Robinson has written a book which will hold the reader's interest, whether a part of the adoption triangle or not. The first part of the book, which portrays her personal life's experiences, reads like a novel. Her own difficult childhood and the ensuing drama of her pregnancy and surrendering of her child finds a resonance in our hearts. In the second part, Ms Robinson sensitively and compassionately explains the tremendous loss experienced by all affected by adoption and suggests ways of dealing with this loss. She also gives an accurate accounting of the manner in which each part of the triangle experiences and responds to adoption reunion. Part 3 contains her own personal and political views of adoption. **I highly recommend this book as a wonderful addition to adoption literature.***

Nancy Newton Verrier, author
The Primal Wound:
Understanding the Adopted Child

Adoption and Loss – *The Hidden Grief*

Adoption and Loss is an important resource for anyone working in the area of adoption and for those whose lives have been personally affected by adoption separation. This book is just as relevant today as it was when it was first written 20 years ago, as the effects of adoption separation don't change . In this new edition, Evelyn's son Ferg has updated the narrative of his experience, which gives us a glimpse into the thoughts and feelings of the adopted person and the challenge and complexity of working out where you fit in the world. Reading both Evelyn's and Ferg's stories, which highlight many unseen challenges and complexities of adoption separation, we begin to understand how fraught the experience of adoption can be. This book contains important and useful insights for everyone who has experienced the impact of adoption in their lives, including adoptive parents. I recommend that this book be compulsory reading for any professionals working in the adoption space and for those supporting people whose lives are affected by adoption.

Nikki Hartmann,
Manager, *Post Adoption Support Service (PASS)*,
South Australia

CONTENTS

Introduction

Ferg's Contribution

PART ONE: Mistreated, mateless mother

     Ch 1 ...in which Evelyn grows up in Renfrew
     Ch 2 ...in which Evelyn moves to Edinburgh
     Ch 3 ...in which Evelyn falls in love
     Ch 4 ...in which Evelyn announces her news
     Ch 5 ...in which Evelyn thinks things over
     Ch 6 ...in which Evelyn waits
     Ch 7 ...in which Evelyn's baby is born
     Ch 8 ...in which Evelyn's baby is taken away
     Ch 9 ...in which Evelyn moves to Bermuda
     Ch 10..in which Evelyn returns to Renfrew
     Ch 11..in which Evelyn moves to Australia
     Ch 12..in which Evelyn tries to find her son
     Ch 13..in which Evelyn discovers the truth
     Ch 14..in which Evelyn contributes

Article :   *Sinking the Mother Ship*

PART TWO: The grief caused by adoption loss

Ch 1   Grief experienced by original mothers
Ch 2   Grief experienced by adopted people
Ch 3   Grief counselling
Ch 4   The silence factor and the role of ritual
Ch 5   Disenfranchised grief
Ch 6   Grief resolution?
Ch 7   Reunion

Article: *The Australian Adoption Apology*

PART THREE: In the 21ˢᵗ Century

Ch 1   Reflections
Ch 2   Consequences
Ch 3   What is adoption?
Ch 4   Does adoption have a future?

Article: *Intercountry adoption - being part of the solution*

Bibliography

National Apology for Forced Adoptions, 21st March 2013

About the author

Adoption and Loss

Introduction

The publication of **Adoption and Loss – *The Hidden Grief*** in Australia in 2000 was a pivotal moment in the history of understanding and acknowledging the long term outcomes of adoption separation. The concepts presented for the first time in this book have been influential not only in Australia, but also in many other locations in which adoptions have taken place. They have been welcomed, endorsed and embraced by those whose lives have been affected by adoption separation and those who care for them, both personally and professionally. In 2000, there was limited access to professional post-adoption support counselling in Australia. At that time the specific features of the loss and grief associated with adoption separation were just beginning to be understood. The message contained in this book has had a significant impact in the last eighteen years.

In the seventh and eighth decades of the twentieth century, in many Western countries, babies born to unmarried women were often taken from their mothers for social reasons and given to married couples to raise. Such adoptions are much less common in the twenty-first century, although loss and grief issues are still experienced when children are adopted for any reason. There are also many family members who are still suffering the long term impact of adoption separation, no matter how many years have passed since the adoption took place.

Adoption and Loss – *The Hidden Grief* came to be written because, in 1996, as a social work student at Flinders University in South Australia, I wrote a 6000 word essay entitled *Grief Associated with the Loss of Children to Adoption*. I discovered while researching this topic that mothers who had lost children through adoption often reported that, not only did time not heal their pain at the loss of their children, but their anger and sense of loss actually *increased* with the passage of time.

This appeared to contradict everything I was being taught about grief resolution. I went on to explore the particular factors which were operating to inhibit grief resolution for those who had experienced adoption separation. Part Two of this book is based on that essay.

Since completing my social work degree, I have invested much time and energy in working to educate politicians, those employed in the helping professions and those whose lives have been affected by adoption separation, in many locations around the world, about the long term impact of disenfranchised grief in relation to adoption separation.

I have also worked to educate members of the community in general, who may have no personal experience of adoption, via my books and my presentations to groups such as the University of the Third Age, Rotary clubs, Probus clubs and YWCA groups, among others.

I presented a paper based on my essay at the Sixth Australian Adoption Conference in Brisbane, Australia in June, 1997. After my presentation, I was approached by one of the workshop presenters at the conference, who said that she was very moved by my paper and asked, *Where can I buy your book?* I replied that I had never written a book. She told me enthusiastically that I should. Many others who heard my presentation or read my paper expressed the same view.

I completed the book in 1998 and submitted it to several publishers. One publisher told me that it was 'not possible' to publish a book about adoption, which combined a personal narrative with an academic exploration of the issues from a professional perspective. When I asked why, the response was, 'Because no one has ever done it before.' I commented that I considered that a very good reason to do it. Few publishers showed any interest in publishing my book and those who did requested major alterations, to which I was not prepared to agree. As a result I decided to self-publish my work.

In the twenty years since I completed the original edition of this book, two very important events in relation to adoption have taken place; one which has particular significance for South Australia and the other which has been very significant for Australia as a whole. I have been privileged to contribute to both of these momentous events. Publishing this updated version of my book has given me the opportunity to include those recent developments, which I believe will be of great interest in all parts of the world where adoption is still practised.

My interest in the long term impact of adoption separation stems from the fact that I am the original mother of a son, who was born in Scotland in 1970 and adopted into another family. I called him Adam, his adoptive parents called him Stephen and he has recently officially named himself Ferg (although I have his permission to continue to call him Stephen). I am very grateful that he has made his own powerful and moving contribution to this book.

The first Adoption Act in Scotland was passed in 1930. Since the passing of that act, adults who have been adopted in Scotland have had the right to access their original birth certificates when they reach adulthood. Because of this, there is no pretence in the birth certificates of children adopted in Scotland. On my son's legal birth certificate, issued in Scotland in 1970, the names of his adoptive parents come under the heading *Names of Adopters*. However, mothers who have been separated from their children by adoption in Scotland have never had a right to access any information about the children they lost to adoption.

In August, 1998 I presented a seminar in Edinburgh at the invitation of the British Association of Social Workers. At this seminar I called for a change to Scottish adoption legislation to allow original parents access to identifying information about their adult, adopted children.

Adoption and Loss

Since 1982, I have lived in South Australia and have been involved with post-adoption issues and services there since 1988. The state of South Australia has had adoption legislation since the passing of the first Adoption Act in 1925. This was later replaced by the *Adoption of Children Act 1967*.

A major review of South Australia's adoption legislation took place in 1987 and was particularly significant. At the time of the review, support groups such as ARMS (Australian Relinquishing Mothers Society), Jigsaw (a support organisation for adults who had been adopted as children and mothers and fathers who had been separated from their children by adoption) and PAG (the Parents of Adoptees Group) lobbied the government to change the Adoption Act to allow for identifying information to be released when the adopted person reached adulthood.

The fact that there were original parents, adults who were adopted as children and adoptive parents, all working together to bring about this major change to adoption legislation was very powerful.

This collaboration was very successful and I should like to express my admiration and appreciation for the politicians who listened to those with a personal experience of the impact of adoption separation and changed the adoption legislation accordingly.

The state of Victoria was the first jurisdiction in Australia to pass legislation, in 1984, to allow adults who had been adopted as children access to their original birth certificates when they reached adulthood. However, with the passing of the *Adoption Act (1988)*, South Australia became **the first jurisdiction in the English-speaking world**, where what are known as 'sealed records' previously existed (that is, where identifying information about the parties to adoption is kept secret) to pass legislation allowing **equal rights** to access identifying information to mothers who had been separated from their children by adoption and adults who had been adopted as children, when the adopted child reaches adulthood. Since that time, similar legislation has been passed throughout Australia.

The South Australian *Adoption Act (1988)* allowed for the release of adoption information under certain conditions. Firstly, no information would be released until an adopted person reached the age of eighteen, unless consent was given by both sets of parents.

Once the adopted person had reached the age of eighteen, that person, or, with their permission, their children, could obtain information relating to the adoption, including the names and addresses of the original parents at the time the adoption took place. At that time, the original mother, or, with her permission, her children, could also obtain information relating to the adoption, including the new identity of the adopted person and the names and address of the adoptive parents at the time of the adoption. Information could also be released to the children after an adopted person or an original mother had died. Original fathers were also able to access information under certain circumstances.

This information could then be used to search in publicly available records. Initially, those who did not wish for their information to be released were given the option to veto its release. I opposed the veto provision for many years and it was finally revoked in 2017.

No more vetoes can be lodged and the existing vetoes are being phased out. All applications for adoption information in South Australia are now processed by the Freedom of Information Team of the Department for Child Protection.

South Australia has set an example to the world. As this pioneering legislation has been operating successfully for **thirty years**, I see no excuse for legislation in other parts of the world where adoptions have taken place not to follow South Australia's inspiring lead. I have contacted many politicians in Scotland over the years, to try to convince them to follow the revolutionary example set by South Australia in 1988. I remain hopeful that those changes will come to pass in my lifetime.

Another significant element of the South Australian *Adoption Act (1988)* is the option for an integrated birth certificate to be issued. Since 1989 (when the *Adoption Act (1988)* came into effect), when a child is adopted, if the original parents and the adoptive parents agree, the details of the adoptive parents can be added to the child's original birth certificate and the original name given to the child, as well as the names of the child's original parents, will not be removed. This document becomes the child's legal birth certificate and it will state that the adopters are the child's legal parents.

The important event which has taken place in South Australia since this book was first published is a recent review of *The Adoption Act*, which took place in 2014 and 2015. The review process allowed members of the community another opportunity to express their views. I, along with many others, made a submission to this review. Those submissions were considered and this resulted in some significant changes to legislation.

The *Adoption (Review) Amendment Act 2016* allows any adult who was adopted in South Australia to apply at any time for an integrated birth certificate, which is that person's legal birth certificate. It contains the names of both the original parents and the adoptive parents.

The new Adoption Act has also made it possible for an adoption order to be discharged (ie reversed). An application can be made for the discharge of an adoption order by 'the adopted person to whom an adoption order relates or a birth parent of the adopted person or an adoptive parent of the adopted person or the Chief Executive'. The grounds for requesting the discharge of an adoption order can be because consent was obtained by fraud, duress or improper means, or because it would be in the best interests of the adopted person.

The Hidden Grief

This means that anyone who has been adopted in South Australia can now reclaim their original name and heritage, which were legally altered by their adoption. Also, a mother who was separated from her child by adoption can also request that the adoption be discharged, if she believes that her consent was obtained by fraud, duress or improper means.

The important event for Australia was that the Australian Senate conducted an enquiry into past adoption experiences, which resulted in a formal apology.

The report of the Australian Senate Enquiry into the Commonwealth Contribution to Former Forced Adoption Policies and Practices was published in 2012. In order to compile the report, members of the Australian Senate had travelled around Australia and consulted with members of the community. They listened to many family members who had been separated by adoption and those who were close to them.

Following the publication of the report, the Australian Government issued a National Apology for Forced Adoptions in 2013, which included the application of federal funding to enhance the post-adoption services which were already available and to allow them to be available to more clients.

I should like to acknowledge the efforts and support of many Australian politicians, who heard and considered with empathy, the submissions from those family members and were responsible for ensuring that the apology was delivered and that it was accompanied by practical support.

I decided to update and republish my first book with the aim of making this information available to a wider audience, in the hope that they could also create opportunities to educate and inform politicians, who will then create positive and beneficial ways to address the long term issues for family members who have been separated by adoption in other parts of the world.

The other reason that I decided to publish this updated version of my first book was that the South Australian

Adoption and Loss

government has announced in the media, via an article in *The Advertiser* newspaper, on the 18th of August, 2018, that they are now implementing a policy of putting in place permanent guardianship orders (known as 'Other Person Guardianship Orders'), which have been available in South Australia since 1993, for children in foster care.

Guardianship is the arrangement that was used in the United Kingdom in the nineteenth century, before legal adoption was introduced, when a child was described as the 'ward' of a guardian. The Oxford Dictionary definition of a 'ward' is: 'a child or young person under the care and control of a guardian appointed by their parents or a court'. Unlike an adoption arrangement, there is no secrecy about the child's origins, no replacement birth certificate and no pretence. The child's heritage and history are respected, because he or she remains legally a member of the family of origin and the original parents of the child are still that child's legal parents. Guardianship is a child-centred outcome, based on honesty and respect.

The Advertiser article stated that the number of children being placed under guardianship orders in South Australia had been steadily increasing, since '…the (g)overnment wrote to eligible foster families and established a central unit to co-ordinate the guardianship process'.

As there are very few adoptions taking place for social reasons in the twenty-first century, it is likely that the current focus on Other Person Guardianship, for children who are unable to live safely with their families of origin, will lead to the phasing out of adoption in South Australia. This has been the goal towards which I have been working for the last twenty years. Children who are unfortunate enough to find themselves unsafe in their family homes deserve the best alternative that we, as a society, can provide for them. A guardianship order gives the child the safety and protection to which they are entitled, without discarding their identity and ancestry.

The Hidden Grief

In the same way that South Australia set an example regarding access to adoption information which has been followed by the rest of Australia and will hopefully eventually be followed by other countries, South Australia is now setting an example by replacing adoption with the more child-centred option of permanent guardianship. Hopefully our enlightened approach will soon be emulated not only by other states and territories in Australia, but also in other countries around the world.

The experiences which I have had and the messages which I have received from readers have served to reinforce for me the views which I have expressed since this book was first published in 2000. I now look back with pride and satisfaction on the events of the last twenty years, which include, in Australia, state and federal government apologies for past adoption separations, as well as an increase in the provision of government funding for post-adoption support services and a decrease in the number of children being adopted.

There has also been progress in other parts of the world in relation to acknowledging the hurt caused by past adoption separations and, to some extent, learning from the mistakes of the past. There have been some significant apologies in Ireland and the Canadian Senate has produced a report entitled *The Shame is Ours - Forced Adoptions of the Babies of Unmarried Mothers in Post-war Canada* and recommended that the Government of Canada issue a formal apology on behalf of all Canadians, to the mothers and their children who were subjected to forced adoption practices in the years following World War II.

In the United Kingdom discussions have also taken place in parliament (thanks to the efforts of MAA – the Movement for an Adoption Apology) about the possibility of following Australia's lead and issuing a government apology for past adoptions. Strenuous efforts are also being made in New Zealand to bring this issue to the attention of government.

Adoption and Loss

My principal aim in writing this book has been to increase awareness and understanding of the loss and the resultant grief experienced by the original mothers of adopted children and the impact of disenfranchised grief on their ability to mourn. I sometimes use the term 'original mother', to describe the woman who has given birth to a child, who was subsequently adopted into another family. It is more convenient than the more precise expression – 'mother who has been separated from her child by adoption'.

The original mother of an adopted child is that child's first mother, the mother who gave birth to the child and the mother from whom the child can trace his or her genetic origins.

What I hope I have made clear with this book is that many of those mothers, regardless of the circumstances surrounding the separation from their children, have suffered grievously from their loss.

I have also explained that their grief is the expected outcome of their experience and that once it has been acknowledged and understood, it can be addressed in an appropriate way and incorporated into their lives.

I have always acknowledged that many fathers who have been separated from their children by adoption have suffered from disenfranchised grief, in the same way that mothers have. In some cases the fathers were not made aware of the pregnancy, in others they were marginalised at the time of the birth. Even when they were able to be involved, their details were often not recorded. This means that if the adult child from whom the father was separated by adoption wants to locate the father, this is often difficult to achieve owing to the lack of identifying information on record.

I have not specifically explored issues for fathers at this time, as I believe that it is more appropriate for fathers themselves to do so. Fathers who have lost children to adoption (such as Gary Coles in Australia and Gary Clapton in Scotland) have produced some interesting and insightful material for those who wish to gain a deeper understanding of their adoption loss issues.

Since I presented my paper in 1997, I have been advised by many adopted people that my explanation of the nature of adoption-related loss and the concept of disenfranchised grief also helped them to understand their own grief at having been adopted. I have also indicated in this book that many adopted people grieve for the loss of their original identities and their original parents and families and that their grief also has been hidden and denied by society.

Other family members, including siblings and grandparents, are often similarly affected. I have also addressed the issue of reunion between family members who have been separated by adoption and the role of reunion in relation to the grieving process.

I believe that my book has relevance for anyone whose life has been affected by adoption separation and that what we have learned from the adoptions which have already taken place should lead us to a future where children who are unable to be raised by their original parents will be cared for by way of arrangements, such as guardianship orders, which are more child-focussed than adoption.

Since I first published this book, many people whose lives have been affected by adoption separation around the world have contacted me to thank me for helping them to understand their experiences.

In the conclusion to the first edition of this book, I stated clearly, *It is time for society to realise that adoption is ethically wrong and morally indefensible ... the way ahead must be a future without adoption*. I have maintained that position steadfastly since that time. It is very satisfying to see my aspiration finally becoming a reality.

Adoption and Loss

This book is in three parts:

Part One, **Mistreated, mateless mother**, is **a** true story of adoption loss. It is my story and it is written from my perspective as the original mother of an adopted child. In it I tell of how I lost my first child through adoption and of the impact which that loss has had on my life.

Part One is followed by an article entitled **Sinking the Mother Ship**, which was written and published in **2012**.

Part Two, **The grief caused by adoption loss**, is what I believe to be **the** true story of adoption loss and its outcomes. It is based on my research as a social work student and my experience as a professional social worker and counsellor. Adoption has caused an enormous amount of grief to a great many people. I do not believe that you can experience an adoption separation without also experiencing the impact of grief. In this part of the book, I address the effects of adoption separation on those involved and the reasons why their grief is not easily resolved. I believe that these two parts of the book complement and validate each other.

Part Two is followed by an article entitled **The Australian Adoption Apology**, which was written and published in **2013**.

In Part Three, **In the 21st Century**, I bring up to date the issues raised in the first two parts. The first two chapters explore the impact of adoption loss in my life and the second two chapters explain why I believe that we will soon see an end to adoption and why this is an admirable goal for Australia and the rest of the world to pursue.

Part Three is followed by **Intercountry Adoption - Being part of the solution**, an article written and published in **2010**.

The Hidden Grief

The book closes with the full text of the **National Apology for Forced Adoptions**, delivered in Canberra, Australia in 2013 by the Hon Julia Gillard, AC, Australia's first female Prime Minister.

I acknowledge with gratitude the efforts of all those family members who have been separated by adoption who have worked generously and honestly to improve understanding of the adoption separation experience and its impact and to support others who have had that experience. I also appreciate the professionals who have taken an interest in adoption separation outcomes and have provided valuable support and understanding.

I should also like to express my thanks to all those friends, colleagues and family members who have encouraged and assisted me to write my books and to educate the world about the long term outcomes of adoption separation. I have laboured to produce nine offspring in my life - five children and four books. I hope that they will all live on after I am gone as my 'after-life'.

Adoption and Loss

The Hidden Grief

Ferg's Contribution

What follows are my recollections, my interpretations and my opinions. Others may disagree with me and/or dispute my memories of certain events. I state them as fact insofar as that's how, from my perspective, I remember certain events. As always, I'm open to and welcome any discussion.

I will use the terms 'adoptive family' and 'original mother' for the sake of consistency.

When you ignore secrets, if you don't resolve them or deal with them, they'll never go away. And sometimes, they'll resurface like a dead body dumped in the water, floating to the surface of a loch, to reignite the ghosts of the past.

Regardless of what position you take in the whole adoption arena I personally believe that all adopted people should search for their families of origin, both on the mother's side and on the father's side. You have a right to know. Don't let other people make that decision for you.

How you do it is up to you of course but whether you should do it has an easy answer in my opinion: YES.

And for the record I don't care who gets upset or uncomfortable by that statement.

If you are an adopted person reading this and you haven't started your journey yet then you may be wrestling with this question: Should I do it, should I search for my original parents and their respective families?

But I suspect the question has already been answered and you're just looking for some piece of information that will support your already made up mind. Hint: return to previous statement above.

Adoption and Loss

Whatever path you choose will inevitably please some people and annoy others just like most things in life.

You may make people angry and upset with your decision or you may unleash a torrent of joy, love, understanding and self-discovery. Or you may have all these reactions and more all at the same time.

Whatever happens in your journey, it is manageable. The world won't end but you will start to see things more clearly and sometimes what comes into focus will pleasantly surprise you. If you get stuck, ask for help. If you don't, onwards and upwards it is.

Ready? Let's go. Here's some of my story.

Introduction:

My name is Ferg Ferguson. At the time of writing I am forty-eight years old. I was born and adopted in Scotland and I currently live in Australia. From an early age I knew I was adopted and I always knew I wanted to find my out about my family of origin, my lineage. It was just a matter of time and circumstance.

I began my search for Evelyn, my original mother, in earnest when I was about nineteen years old. At that time I was living in Scotland and she was in Australia. If you believe in fate then our reunion story will have you smiling and nodding for years to come.

I won't lie, there have been casualties along the way. Some of those casualties were necessary and desirable. For example, many of the old ideas and assumptions I had about who I was, about my adoptive family and my attitudes to certain things all 'died'.

I see these 'deaths' as the positive outcome of my journey, for in their place stands a shiny, new, better informed Ferg.

Other casualties were painful to lose. Their loss was the inevitable consequence of a life lived with honesty and integrity and of asking others to do the same. Sacrifices had to be made: I view mine as cutting off a diseased branch to save the tree it was threatening to infect.

Overall though, the prize at the end was most definitely worth all the effort. Without question.

How my feelings about adoption have changed over the years:

It's hard for me to give an objective view on adoption in general without my own biases seeping into the narrative. I can see how in its most simplistic form the idea of so-called 'unwanted' children being given to parents who want to rear a child, so much so that any child will serve the purpose, would have sounded like a great idea at the time.

How the limited understanding, at that time in society, of the infant mind would allow you no trepidation in handing over one woman's baby to a complete stranger and thinking that young person's life would be without issues or problems or uncomfortable questions following on from that decision.

Then there's the value judgements attached to the idea of 'providing a better life' for a child. One need only look at Aboriginal Australia's history of The Stolen Generation to see how that panned out. Take out the racism and that idea is still fraught with a great many difficulties.

On top of all that, there's the 'forget about it and move on' camp. I have been told this many times by my own adoptive family when I tried to explore some of the difficulties I was experiencing in my teenage mind as I grappled with the ever increasing list of unanswered questions in my head.

Mothers who'd lost children to adoption were told it by medical professionals, friends and family and society in general.

It is as useless as it is ignorant to tell someone 'forget about it and move on'. That might work for your son or daughter recently dumped by their boyfriend or girlfriend but not for a child separated from his/her mother.

Adoption and Loss

When I was growing up in my adoptive family I never considered myself to have any problems in relation to the adoption because I was able to think about, analyse, dissect and explore all the issues in my own head and not feel damaged or over burdened by any of it. The only problem I had was trying to engage my adoptive parents in the exploration.

Only with age, hindsight and appropriate counselling can I look back and analyse what my life was really like. If my 'good adoption story' was actually nothing of the sort then what must somebody else's story which they labelled 'bad' or negative be like? I dread to think.

But this begs the question: Is there such a thing as a good adoption story at all? How many people are hurt and displaced psychologically by one woman's baby being raised by another woman? 'Lots' is the answer as we often forget about the siblings, grandparents, aunts, uncles, etc who are also affected by the loss of a child.

And that damage, while not irreparable for some, can still last a lifetime and then go on to affect many more people who are now connected to that adopted person.

It wasn't until I became an adult and started to go to counselling, brought on by the sudden death of my adoptive father, that I began the process of looking back at my life and seeing some of the psychological results of my own adoption.

The 'small "t" trauma' as the counsellor labelled it I had been experiencing throughout my life had been buried in my psyche. Much of it was a result of pushback from my adoptive parents as they struggled (badly) to contain my desire for self-knowledge and then had to watch their secrets and lies begin to unravel.

I always thought I'd had a happy and loving family environment but if my newly released traumas were anything to go by then that was a lie I'd told myself in order just to muddle through.

It turns out that my 'happy adoption story' wasn't so happy after all.

The Hidden Grief

When I was a child:

When I was a young child at school, in Primary One, aged approximately six years old, my teacher wrote at the bottom of my school report card in the comment section: 'Unusually depressed for such a small child.'

I don't really remember that far back and have no clear recollection of feeling depressed. When I found this report card as a young adult it took me by surprise. However, it suggested all was not well in my young mind. Was it because I was in the wrong family? I don't know. Was I suffering due to the separation? It looks that way.

As hard as I tried I couldn't forget that comment and returned to it many times as I grew up, much to the discomfort of my adoptive parents. Then one day when I asked again I was told by my adoptive mother: "I've thrown it out to make room in the cupboard."

How much extra room did you save by chucking out my one page report card? Why didn't you just give it to me to store at my house? Silence, was the answer. Forget about it and move on, was the underlying message. And if you can't do that for yourself then we will damn well do it for you.

Another 'small "t" trauma' burrowed down into my emotional self. It wouldn't be the last time my adoptive parents made such decisions for me without telling me at the time.

Around the age of seven or eight I was told that I had been adopted. That my mother wasn't my real mother. Apparently unperturbed I had simply accepted the fact and went outside to play football.

Out there with my friends I started to tell people my new story. They were my friends and neighbours, we shared things. Word eventually got back to my adoptive parents who were angry with me that I'd told people.

Adoption and Loss

They didn't want anyone to know but I didn't see why we had to lie. The seeds had been sown and their shoots were beginning to grow.

Looking for Evelyn:

I had been thinking about my family of origin all throughout my life. Feelings waxed and waned as my teenage years took over. I had started to deliver newspapers and magazines as a part time job before and after school and on the weekends just after turning fifteen years old.

I used to read all the magazines for free before delivering them to my customers, one of the perks of the job. It was during one of my readings of the weekly 'problem page' answers in a popular women's magazine that I stumbled across someone else looking for advice on how to find their original family. The 'Agony Aunt' replied with contact details of a relevant organisation for the person to contact for further help.

I took down these details and promised myself I would give them a call soon thereafter.

As I quickly found out however, living at home in a terraced council house offers you little to no privacy as a teenager. Neither of my adoptive parents worked so there was always someone in the house, day and night. We had two rotary dial telephones: one in the dining room which was part of our open plan ground floor and the other was in my parents' bedroom.

I was finding it almost impossible to get the privacy I needed to make such a phone call and take notes from it. Or to receive any letters or mail without someone else either opening it and reading it while I wasn't there and then asking awkward questions, or enquiring why I was getting mail from 'Blah Blah Adoption Services'. I wasn't sure what I wanted to do with any information I received at that point so it was important for me to not have anyone else know what I was looking for at that stage. Telling everyone later was always part of my plan however.

The Hidden Grief

As this was such a private thing to do I wanted control over any information I uncovered and over any choices I made later.

I grew up in a new town built in the 1970s called Cumbernauld on the outskirts of Glasgow city. I knew I'd be going to university after school and that meant moving out of the family home into the city. This meant eventually having my own flat and with that came the privacy I needed.

So I kept the contact details of the organisation and promised myself that as soon as I got my own place I would start the journey to try and find my family of origin.

The motivation to search is difficult to explain. It feels so natural to me. How do you explain the motivation of wanting to know your absent flesh and blood to someone who already lives with theirs? To me it doesn't need explanation. It's almost impossible. I imagine it would be like a woman trying to explain the feeling of pregnancy to a man.

I didn't find out until later on, during our first reunion together, that Evelyn had, through the third party who'd arranged the adoption (the Mormon Church), twice contacted my adoptive parents looking to speak to me. She was threatened angrily with legal action and told not to get in touch ever again.

My adoptive parents had point blank refused to tell me or talk to me about it. Choices about my life were made in secret, behind my back, for me. The first time this happened I was about fifteen or sixteen years old, the excuse being that as I was sitting important school exams it was best not to disturb me or my studies, I later found out. They colluded in lying to me by omission. The secrets and lies began to pile up.

Evelyn didn't heed those first warnings and tried to contact me again a few years later while she was on holiday in Scotland in 1989. Again, my adoptive parents withheld this from me. And again, they threatened her and this time The Mormon Church too.

Sometime around 1990 I moved into my own flat in the West End of Glasgow. As most young people are, I was relieved that I could now do everything by myself and didn't have to explain anything to anybody. Nobody looking over my shoulder as I read letters, nobody listening to what I was saying on the phone.

So I started to search. It was hard but exciting work. Each new phone call brought another new lead to follow. I was slowly putting pieces together that I'd hoped would finally allow me to meet my biological family. Documents were opened for the first time in years, names and places were pored over for connections. I was getting closer by the day but then suddenly I hit a brick wall. The trail went completely cold and the information dried up.

I spoke with a guy in Glasgow City Council somewhere who had agreed to meet me in his office to discuss where to go next. He told me that someone had requested my file in another office and would I be able to pick it up on the way down to see him. "No problem" said I and set off down the road near my flat to grab it.

It was now the beginning of 1991 and unbeknown to me a counsellor in Glasgow that Evelyn was in touch with from Australia had then contacted my adoptive parents again. She apparently phoned the number on the file and started talking to the male voice on the other end of the phone thinking it was me. It was my adoptive father and he was livid.

He talked about taking legal action of some kind if the agency ever contacted him in the future and when the adoption counsellor asked my adoptive parents if they would please ask me to speak to her (as I was an adult at this time) they said that 'they would not and that they didn't need to ask me, they knew without asking me that I wasn't interested at all.'

They did release some very limited general information about me and how I was getting on in life on the understanding that now Evelyn had some knowledge of me and that everything was alright in my life then she would have no reason to contact them again, seeing as the repeated angry threats from before obviously hadn't worked to keep her away.

The Hidden Grief

A few weeks after that phone call, the very person Evelyn and the counsellor had been looking for, namely: me, walked into that same counsellor's office to pick up my adoption file on my way to the guy who was going to help me try to find my original mother.

The woman nearly had a heart attack on the spot.

Soon thereafter Evelyn and I spoke on the phone for hours. I could do this now in private in my own flat.

She said she was paying for a return flight to visit her in Australia which I excitedly accepted.

Now it was time to tell my adoptive parents my news. I returned to the family home to sit them down to explain what was happening. I didn't know at that time Evelyn had already tried to contact me twice because that had been hidden from me.

A massive verbal fight broke out culminating in me being called all sorts of bad names. Amongst other things I was called a liar and accused of betraying them. I tried in vain to get them to understand why I needed to search for my biological family but it all fell on deaf ears.

At no point during those heated discussions did they tell me that she had already tried to contact me twice before that time. I only found this out later while talking to Evelyn in Australia.

The double standard stuck in my throat for many years. The narrative was that I'd betrayed them for searching for then finding my original mother then coming home to sit them down as adults to tell them face to face. Their betrayal by hiding all those attempts at contact from me was simply ignored. My so-called betrayal was the focus, they never admitted to theirs. All the while calling me names accusing me of doing the very same thing that they had done to me but were still hiding from me.

I'm not actually sure if I ever truly got over that hypocrisy. Unfortunately it was not the last time my adoptive parents did something like that to me.

Adoption and Loss

I'm often curious about what my life would have turned out like if I had been told at the time that Evelyn was trying to make contact and supported through that if need be?

One of the things that upsets me most about those decisions to keep that information from me is that I was never given the option of deciding anything for myself. Other people decided who I should know and not know. My choice was not important.

After I met Evelyn and the family:
Meeting someone new is always going to be a gamble. Like going on a blind date but with a potential lifetime connection attached. I was excited and open to the idea of meeting as many people as I could.

It's difficult to describe what it feels like exactly and of course everyone will be different and every situation will be different to mine. I had missing pieces of the grand jigsaw of who I was and meeting Evelyn and the rest of her family filled in a lot of them for me.

I was relieved more than anything else I think after I returned home to Scotland. There are so many possible outcomes from a meeting of this kind but I felt fortunate that my original mother and I were very similar in a lot of ways.

I felt a genuine connection with her at that time and knew that I wanted to stay in touch and explore our new relationship. I'm so glad I did.

The impact it had on my life however was massive, mostly positive but there were some negatives, on the surface at least.

Growing up, I didn't particularly feel like I was broken or missing something that only meeting my original mother would fill; that wasn't what drove my search. You are missing something, of course, but when I heard stories from other adopted people I didn't feel like I related to their kind of negative characterisation.

The Hidden Grief

I always approached the situation as adding something interesting to my life rather than filling in a hole where something was missing.

Searching for my original mother, finding her then visiting and integrating her and her family into my life caused irreparable damage to my relationship with my adoptive family in Scotland. My adoptive father just couldn't handle it. He got progressively worse and angrier with me for a variety of things in my life. The name calling got nastier and the relationship broke down. We didn't speak for many years and to be honest I welcomed the break from his verbal abuse. My adoptive mother's passive aggressiveness continued unabated. I never heard much condemnation of my adoptive father's stance from her, just a silent acceptance.

My life with my adoptive family became riddled with arguments, name calling, lies and emotional distance all as a consequence of that desire to know who and where I came from. It seems such a small thing to want to know yet it caused me a great many problems.

Looking on the bright side however, positively it has given me many wonderful gifts. It's difficult to properly articulate how exciting it is other than to say that it gives me a sense of belonging that I later realised wasn't there for most of my life growing up in a different family.

I was never close to my younger adoptive brother for a variety of reasons. After meeting my original family I found I had four new blood related siblings: two half-brothers and two half-sisters. As with any family, bonds with various members differ and can change over time of course but I quickly felt much more connected to my sisters for some reason once we were all old enough to know each other as young adults. That strong bond continues today.

Adoption and Loss

Living as an authentic human being should not be something you have to fight for. That means, if possible, being in charge of your own life and making your own informed choices.

I just wanted to live honestly in the world with nothing to hide. To tell the absolute truth about where I came from and how I came to be the person I am today. To understand my history and past and how it affects who I am now and potentially who I am going to be in the future. To know who my blood relatives are and to share in their life if we both choose to.

Fear and secrets are destructive, honesty and openness are empowering.

As I matured leading up to the counselling:

Not long after I had met Evelyn for the first time, in 1991, I was keen to read more about adoption and the psychological issues involved. Because she was researching the effects on other women who had lost their children to adoption too she had access to a wide and interesting range of reading material.

She gave me a copy of a book called: ***The Primal Wound*** by Nancy Verrier, around the time I was twenty-three, so sometime in 1993 or 94. One particular chapter, chapter seven, discussed issues of rejection, trust, intimacy and loyalty. This chapter had a profound effect on me not only at the time but continuing on today, some twenty-five years later.

In a nutshell, the chapter explored the idea that, generally speaking, male adoptees have difficulty maintaining long term romantic relationships with females *because* they were adopted. The idea is that without proper acceptance and then counselling, the adult male falls into a pattern of sabotaging adult relationships with females because any such relationship reminds them of the time they were trying to bond with their original mother and that bond was forcibly broken, causing pain and suffering in the baby or young child's mind.

The Hidden Grief

To protect the adult psyche from the threat of the same thing happening again, the subconscious mind recognises the bond beginning and either breaks it pre-emptively or sabotages it soon after in order to protect the host from the pain of the bond being broken sometime later, when it is undoubtedly stronger, as happened with their original mother.

I used to pride myself on my ability to escape being tied down by a long term relationship with a female. And, being a non-religious person and someone who does not believe in fate, I also believed that we humans are in charge of our own destiny, that we have choice and free will and that there is no great God-made plan for our lives that we cannot change (this is the simple version).

I was always interested in psychology, even before meeting Evelyn and was aware of the subconscious mind and how it could affect your behaviour in certain ways without your conscious mind having much say over that, so to speak.

When presented with the issue in chapter seven of me potentially sabotaging my own relationships and not being in control of that, I initially fought against it. This idea was completely undermining everything I thought I knew about myself and why I did things or chose to do things. It did not sit well with me at all so I went into denial. I fought for control and for the idea that I was in control of my decisions, not some part of my subconscious mind reacting to something which happened when I was just a baby.

Around ten years later in 2005 when presenting my personal story at a small adoption meeting in Melbourne with Evelyn, I broached the subject again, wondering out loud how you could tell the difference between which part of your brain was making a decision: the conscious mind or the subconscious mind?

Fast forward to now, in 2018, and after much thought on the subject and a fair bit of counselling with a specialist mental health social worker, I'm still not sure how to tell the difference. But at least I am accepting now of the idea that subconscious 'baby Ferg' may well be disturbing conscious life for 'adult Ferg', whether he wants him to or not. How to tell the difference is still outside of my mental grasp for now but I'll definitely keep working on it.

So, to all my past girlfriends whose romantic relationships with me ended abruptly or without proper explanation, I sincerely apologise as it is entirely possible that it was 'baby Ferg' doing the loudest talking in my head. Most probably it had nothing to do with you at all.

I never fully understood the damage and disorientation that can occur in a person's life after they are adopted into a new family. I have felt it quite acutely at times and that's what prompted me to seek out answers from both my adoptive family and in the relevant literature.

I was naive, some might say overly optimistic, to think that others would share my zeal for such psychological exploration.

Doing new things, travelling to new places, exploring the unknown always filled me with excitement. They all still do. So in that respect I haven't changed at all. Jumping straight into the deep end, into the unknown electrifies me (in the best possible way).

My search for answers has often brought me into conflict with those who don't want to share them so I was always used to having to fight for certain positions or look for more creative ways to solve a problem.

As I look back at my life now I have come to see how much more damaging being adopted can actually be. Particularly so if you have an adoptive family such as I had, one who wanted to shut down my exploration and questions at every turn.

It was uncomfortable for them to think about those possibilities and they reacted quite aggressively at times. This caused me a lot of unresolved grief.

A lot of their behaviour was borne from a deep seated insecurity too, that they would 'lose me to her' or that 'she didn't deserve to have me in her life because she gave me away'.

The Hidden Grief

These barbs hurt me even though they were not directed at me *per se*.

These last twenty years or so have taught me the value of family and shown me how terrible it can be for a child or adult searching for their original family, more so if the caretaker family actively tries to hide contact from them in the process.

Obviously the bond is much deeper for me as I was going to search no matter what. And even after the fights it caused I did not waver, in fact it probably drove me to assert myself more strongly.

It's very sad that my adoptive family fought so hard to deny me my most basic human desire: to know who I am and where I came from.

And also to deny Evelyn's right too: to know her own son. Signing a piece of paper and giving a baby a new name does not change that fundamental drive for self-knowledge. For some, like me, it only magnifies it.

I always tried to talk about my feelings, to explore where they came from and to try and analyse what was happening in my brain. Psychology intrigued me at university and I was eager to apply that knowledge to my own situation of being adopted.

My adoptive parents were the complete opposite to that; they never discussed feelings and quickly sought to shut down any exploration I wanted to go on. Were they scared? Were they even equipped with the tools to properly traverse such an unknown emotional landscape? I don't know for sure but the reaction was always the same: I was silenced and they did everything in their power to prevent me from going there.

Changing my name:
Growing up I was called 'Fergy', my nickname derived from the shortening of my adoptive family name of Ferguson. On entering my teenage years this changed into 'The Ferg Man' which was later pruned down to just 'Ferg'. I've since always been known as and introduced to friends, parents, teachers, lecturers, etc just as

Adoption and Loss

'Ferg'. I remember people at my first university graduation ceremony remarking that they never knew my full name (Stephen Miller Ferguson) when it was announced for me to receive my degree on stage.

When I was born Evelyn named me Adam George Burns. On being adopted six days later my adoptive family named me Stephen Miller Ferguson.

Even though I have lived outside of Scotland for many years I still maintain strong friendships there and travel back to hook back into my home culture whenever I can.

A few years ago while back visiting friends in Scotland I decided to change my name by deed poll. After the formalities, a long time good friend and I travelled through to Edinburgh to pick up my new birth certificate.

Although it was initially done 'for a bit of a laugh' I got this strange feeling of ownership back. I hadn't expected to feel this way at all so it was quite a surprise to me. My new name is now Ferg Ferguson.

Another thing that surprised me was the strength of the negative reaction from my adoptive parents (again). I guess in hindsight I should have seen it coming, primarily because most of my life choices have attracted a similar level of reaction from them over the years: subjects chosen to study at university, lifestyle choices, my apparent sexuality (wrongly labelled I might add), my appearance (tattoos and piercings bringing some monumental fights and verbal abuse my way), countries to which I liked to travel, number of girlfriends, the list goes on and on.

Whatever I did never really felt like it was good enough for them so of course the new name I chose for myself wasn't either. It was turned into another perceived attack on them: "How could you do such a thing without asking us?" (I was 45 years old), and then the guilt trip: "We gave you a nice name, why would you want to change it into that?!" and then the disempowerment: "I don't care what you change it to, I'm calling you what I want, Stephen….you can't make me call you Ferg."

Since I was born then lost to adoption at six days old I have been the unwitting victim of a fight for control, an emotional tug of war between my original mother and my adoptive mother. This is the outcome for every adopted child.

Some will know and be aware of that as I was from the moment I sat my adoptive parents down and told them I'd searched for, found and was going to visit my original mother in Australia.

Others will be unaware of both sides' dreams, desires and basic needs and wants.

This might also explain a wee bit about why adopted people often report feeling guilty for existing, this constant pull both ways which can illicit strong feelings of divided loyalties forever unresolved, as I personally have felt for much of my life.

I love my new name and by the amounts of compliments I get for it, so do many others.

Being disowned and then cut out of the will:

I can't write about my journey without mentioning this. It was the lightning bolt from the blue which almost destroyed me. But in actuality it saved me because it pushed me into counselling.

Sometime after my name change my adoptive father, mother and brother got together and all co-signed a new version of my adoptive father's will. His health was failing and I imagine he thought he'd be first to die.

I don't know for sure what prompted it but he had been searching for me on the Internet apparently and found a copy of the old presentation I'd done in 2005 with Evelyn which was written for an audience at post-adoption services.

In that presentation there were a number of statements relating to adoption in general and my long running battles with my adoptive family to try and understand it that he obviously didn't like being reminded of. Because our family never spoke about these kinds of things I only found this out much later through my adoptive mother.

Angry, he had officially disowned me and then had written me out of his will. As usual nobody told me this had happened. More family secrets.

Looking back, none of what was in that presentation would have been news to my adoptive father or the rest of the family. It was really just an overview for a new audience of my struggles with them to understand adoption and my place in the world because of it.

While I was back in Scotland a couple of years ago at Christmas time to help tend to his ailing health and to assist in his transition from hospital to home, he suddenly died.

He died on the bedroom floor as I was giving him CPR.

My adoptive mother wasn't able to fix all the finances and things you have to do when someone dies and my adoptive brother, well let's just say that kind of stuff was better left in my hands. This is how and when I found out about the will.

His untimely death made sure they were forced to tell me what they had done with the will as I was tasked with tidying up the family expenses for my adoptive mother on his passing.

She tried desperately to cover up the gaping hole right in front of us, claiming "she didn't know where the will was in the house", that "there were more important things to be thinking about", and "never mind it's just a normal will" etc but eventually she had to give in and show it to me.

She started to cry and told me that "she wished she had died instead as it wasn't fair that she was the one who had to sit here and tell me what they'd done", again, behind my back.

The same feelings of anger, betrayal and disempowerment burst out and for a moment I thought I was going to completely break apart.

At that point I knew that my relationship with my adoptive family, or what was left of it, was over.

The Hidden Grief

That they were willing to do such a thing to me again as an adult and got caught again trying to hide it, showed me their true feelings towards me. It was calculated and deliberate and they had all worked together to keep it from me.

There was no: 'That was wrong, sorry we shouldn't have done that' or 'Let me go down to the lawyers and fix that, now that it's my will'.

They had all been waiting for me to return to Australia after getting my adoptive father back safely into the family home and were most likely never going to tell me, leaving me to find out once someone had died in the future and I was safely halfway round the world, too far away to get back in time to see the will. Someone else would have fixed things by then. Unfortunately for them I just happened to be there and in charge of the finances when he died unexpectedly.

And to answer your question (and some of my friends'): No, I still don't believe in Karma.

I genuinely don't care about half of a house, it's the behaviour, the same secrets and lies right up to the end that upset me the most.

Lying to me by omission about my original mother trying to contact me then lying to me again when you cut me out of your will like that: is that something I should put up with, again?

The truth is we're all fools for love and approval because our insecurities shout so much louder than rational thought. If someone treats us badly, the easiest thing in the world is to allow their behaviour to merely confirm our own poor opinion of ourselves.

I'm not the first and I won't be the last person to make excuses for a parent who has brought you down so low you believe it's your destiny to survive on scraps of affection.

But it's not good enough to act like a bystander in your own emotional life. 'Oh but it's family', only stretches so far. Emotional abuse is emotional abuse no matter who it comes from. The trick is to recognise it as such and get as far away from it as you safely can, to protect yourself, heal and then move on with your life.

I made the conscious choice that I don't have space in my life for people like that any more, family or not.

I no longer have or want any contact with what's left of my adoptive family so I told them, politely and then wished them good luck as I walked away, for good.

Not only was it lying, it was controlling and while I can't stop people lying to me, I can stop people controlling me.

I don't feel like a victim, I simply feel free.

It's easy to lose sight of how much easier life becomes when you take charge of your destiny and make your own choices. When you stop being controlled and start being in control.

There's no excuse for settling for less than you deserve, especially when 'what you deserve' is just common decency, honesty and respect.

The impact of the counselling, a game changer:

It usually takes some catastrophic event or reaction for people to admit they need psychological help. Mine was not just the death of my adoptive father while I was giving him CPR on the bedroom floor, it was what happened after that.

The counselling I am having, brought on by his death, has literally blown me away. I cannot speak highly enough of it.

I felt as though I'd been struck by lightning. In that one moment I literally felt completely and utterly out of control. I had never experienced such a visceral reaction to anything before in my whole life. Therefore, to fully understand what was going on I needed help.

After the funeral and on my return to Australia I was put in touch with a specialist mental health professional who dealt a lot with adoption issues and came highly recommended by post-adoption services.

The Hidden Grief

I, like many other people no doubt, liked to think of myself as mentally strong and able to deal with what the world could throw at me. Going to see a counsellor was an admission of failure, of sorts.

At the beginning (and it turns out somewhat naively) I didn't feel like I had much to complain about. I thought I was there only to deal with the feelings and reactions following my adoptive father's death, tied into the issues around the will.

Like pulling on an errant thread at the edge of an old rug, a short bit of exploration of my life from the counsellor and my happy, slightly guarded demeanour began to totally unravel. Previously buried traumas soon came pouring out. And then some.

I had the strange sensation of sitting opposite this wee woman I'd just met and crying. Not only was I crying, but I found myself being so overcome with emotion that I literally couldn't speak. My brain was sending messages to my mouth to say something but my mouth was unable to make any sounds.

Talk about losing control!

All I could do was sit as some passive observer of myself while my body did something different to what it was being told to do. If I hadn't experienced it for myself I would have had trouble believing that something like this could really happen to me.

This experience has changed me forever. Infinitely for the better. In fact I'm still in awe at the power of what happened.

Obviously I had a lot of unresolved work to do, so I asked her to take me deeper into the recesses of my mind to find out what else was in there. Indiana Jones would have been excited with an adventure such as this one.

It appears that I have been soaking up a lifetime worth of negative emotions during and because of my adopted life and not dealing with them properly at the time.

These 'small "t" traumas' collected over the years until the post-death counselling brought them all back to the surface in one big wave, explains why I felt so utterly helpless in that moment.

Adoption and Loss

Because I hadn't acknowledged them before I was unprepared to deal with my reaction when they reappeared. Hence the trip to the counsellor.

With every acknowledgement of a trauma and then working through it with a professional, healing can begin. To find out how well you are progressing, revisit the trauma and if you have no reaction to it, for example no more tears, no more debilitating (and freaky) inability to speak, no more sweaty palms or butterflies in the stomach then you're well on the way to snuffing out its power over you in the future.

I felt immediately lighter as I was exorcising my own wee demons which I'd collected and locked away somewhere in my brain.

I have a much better picture now of who I am and who I was and what actions contributed to creating those traumatic events in my life.

I am much happier and encouraged by the work I was able to do with my counsellor. I can't praise her highly enough.

Those little trauma 'monsters' have no hold over me any more. I can cut them loose from my life and not worry if they do find a way back in. They can't harm me or control me now, they have lost all their power.

I came out of those sessions and immediately told a number of friends all about what had happened, so enthused was I.

I also saw in them traumas of their own which were affecting parts of their life negatively. I haven't yet stopped encouraging them to seek counselling too. They definitely need some from where I'm standing, in fact we all probably do.

If there is one last message I would like to give the readers of this book it is this:

It saddens me that my adoptive family reacted in the way they did but I do not regret for one moment the decision I made to seek out my biological family.

Having them in my life is a wonderful experience and one I wouldn't change for any one.

The Hidden Grief

The journey itself is the win, the outcome is forever changing and growing, thankfully in the right direction for us all.

For those adopted people who haven't searched yet: DO IT NOW.

For those who've searched and it brings you difficulties: WORK ON THEM AND GET COUNSELLING.

For those who've searched and it brings you the same joy it has brought me: WELL DONE, NOW HELP OTHERS LESS FORTUNATE THAN YOURSELF REACH THEIR GOALS.

For those working in post-adoption services and counselling: A HUGE THANK YOU.

For those mothers (and fathers) who gave birth to us: DON'T GIVE UP, WE LOVE YOU FROM AFAR.

For those adoptive parents who want to shut down, silence, lie to and control their adopted child: TRY WORKING TOGETHER WITH THEM OPENLY AND HONESTLY. THIS WILL STRENGTHEN YOUR BOND, NOT WEAKEN IT.

Ferg Ferguson
October 2018
Happy to be contacted on **ferg70@gmail.com**

Adoption and Loss

Part One

Mistreated, mateless mother

Adoption and Loss

Chapter 1 ... in which Evelyn grows up in Renfrew

I was born towards the end of 1949 and raised in Renfrew, a small town on the outskirts of Glasgow, Scotland. Renfrew has been there, on the banks of the River Clyde, since the twelfth century. In the twentieth century, this stretch of the river was the heart of the Scottish shipbuilding industry.

My parents were engaged when the Second World War broke out. My paternal grandmother said to my mother, *You'd better marry him in case he has to go to war. Then if he gets killed you'll get a War Widow's Pension. If you're not married, you'll get nothing.* They married in November, 1939 and my father was called up almost immediately. He spent the next six years in Iceland, North Africa and Italy, coming home occasionally on leave and managing thereby to father two children. My mother worked in a munitions factory.

The Clyde area was bombed heavily during the war because of the shipyards. In Clydebank, which lies directly across the river from Renfrew, only seven houses were left undamaged after the Blitz. When the war ended in 1945, prefabricated homes were built, as they were cheap and easy to erect. My parents moved, with my brother and sister, into a 'prefab' and began their life together as a married couple, *six years after their wedding.* After the war, my father trained as a typewriter mechanic with

Adoption and Loss

Remington Rand. Consequently, when I started school I didn't recite 'A, B, C, D, E' like the other children. Instead my alphabet began with 'Q, W, E, R, T'.

Many years later, looking back over his life, my father said to me, *Hitler ruined my life*. He told me that when he came back from the war, he struggled to find his place in society and in his family. The family had grown and developed without him. My mother, like many women at that time, had learned to cope without a man and had been running the household efficiently in his absence. My father, on the other hand, had spent those six years in the army, taking orders. His children were strangers to him. Returning to his wife and children after the war, he felt redundant.

When I was born, my father had no experience of being a father to a young child. I do not recall spending a great deal of time with my father throughout my childhood. In those days it was not common for fathers to play an active role in their children's upbringing. However, from my earliest years, I felt that my father resented me. I spent a large part of my life trying to work out why.

With hindsight, I believe that he actually resented all three of his children to some extent, as they competed with him for my mother's attention, affection and time. Because of the war, they had not been able to enjoy their early married life together, before the arrival of children, as most couples do. I remember no hugs, no warmth or affection from my father. The only time we ever spent together was when he taught me to play cribbage. He was happy to have the occasional game with me until, at the age of twelve, I was finally able to win a game against him. He never played a game of cribbage with me again. However, I'm glad that he took the time to teach me and I still play a mean game of crib, if I do say so myself.

As a child, I spent a lot of time alone, since my brother and sister were both several years older than I was. They were

The Hidden Grief

both at school before I was born. By the time I started primary school, my sister was in high school and by the time I started high school, my sister had left home.

My mother worked in my pre-school years and my grandmother looked after me. This was unusual in the 1950s, a time when most mothers were full-time carers. The reason that my mother worked, I discovered when I was older, was because my father had an over-fondness for drinking and gambling and my mother had to work to supplement the small and irregular amounts of housekeeping money that he gave her.

My mother suffered from a heart condition and had been told by her doctor not to work. She visited him for regular check-ups and always lied to him, denying that she was working. I recall one child very mysteriously telling me that she knew why my mother was the first person in our street to have a washing machine. It was because the doctor had told her that, with her heart condition, she shouldn't be washing by hand. I was terrified. I thought that my mother might die at any minute.

My father was always employed, never took sick leave and was never late for work. At weekends, however, he was frequently intoxicated. I became aware as I grew up that the neighbours talked about us. Other children teased me about my father's drinking and about the fact that my mother worked. That made me feel that we were in some ways inferior to other families.

My mother actually worked in a range of environments until she was in her sixties. When her children were still living at home, she worked part-time in order to be able to combine her role as a mother with her employment commitments. In my opinion, compared to many women of her generation, who conformed to social expectations and spent their lives looking after the home and family, my mother's experience in the workforce contributed to her becoming a well-rounded, balanced and altogether interesting person.

Adoption and Loss

Apart from these tensions, our little community of prefabs was generally a very safe, friendly one. At least, we felt safe at the time. Environmentally, it was perhaps not the healthiest place to raise children. At one end of our street was the gasworks, at the other end a huge electricity pylon.

As a child I read a lot. There were always books in the house, not because my parents bought them, but because, at that time, books were given as awards at school for good results or good attendance. Books were also given at Sunday School and Boys' Brigade in recognition of various achievements. I read everything that came into the house and was as interested in *What Katy Did* as I was in what happened down *King Solomon's Mines*. We also owned a beautiful set of encyclopaedias, with which I spent many happy hours. I had plenty of opportunity to read, as I was a rather solitary child and was frequently absent from school in winter due to recurrent bouts of tonsillitis.

I remember my mother as, above all, kindly and generous. As a child, I often came home to find door-to-door salesmen of various nationalities sitting at our kitchen table, eating Mum's homemade soup. We lived in the prefab, my sister, brother and I sharing a bedroom, until I was ten years old. Then we moved into a larger house, which we shared with my maternal grandmother.

I attended the Blythswood Testimonial School, which was opened in 1843. I was a quick learner and completed primary school, after six years instead of seven, at the age of eleven. Because I had done so well, my headmaster, Mr Mackay, was keen for me to take up the opportunity of an academic education. He felt that I had the potential to 'make something of myself'. My father refused to give permission.

His belief, shared by many working-class parents at the time, was that I should 'know my place' and not 'get ideas above my station'. His plan was to get me out into the workforce as soon as possible. Besides, my sister and brother had not had the advantage of an extended education and so why should I think that

The Hidden Grief

I deserved any better than they did. I actually had no particular preference at the time. My mother defied him and agreed to send me to Paisley Grammar School, against his wishes. From the time that I started high school, my father became even more distant.

From the age of fifteen, I was the only child left at home and I had a sense that my father longed to have his wife to himself again, as he did for a very brief time after their marriage.

Paisley Grammar School was founded by Royal Charter of James VI, King of Scotland, on the 3rd of January 1576 and had a proud tradition of providing a quality education. I spent six years there, but, coming from a working class background, I always felt somewhat out of place. In spite of that, I worked hard to make the most of the opportunity which my mother had created for me. I believe that a good education should produce young adults who have learned analytical thinking and empathy, qualities of which one can never have enough. I was fortunate to have been able to develop those qualities during my time at Paisley Grammar and have drawn on them to write my books.

After my higher exams, in my fifth year of high school, I was the top student in French and was awarded the French prize (*Les Miserables* by Victor Hugo, in French, of course). My parents didn't attend the prize giving. I have a vivid memory of obtaining my Scottish Certificate of Education higher results and proudly sharing them with my mother, who congratulated me on my achievement and encouraged me to show them to my father. I was reluctant, but she was confident that he would be proud of me. His only comment was, *Was that the best you could do?* I replied defiantly with, *Yes, it was, actually!* His question rang in my ears for many years to come.

Chapter 2 ... in which Evelyn moves to Edinburgh

I had no idea what I was going to do when I left school. Some of my friends were going to university. I assumed that we couldn't afford a university education. Then a friend told me that it didn't cost anything and that government grants were available. I knew that my parents wanted me out in the workforce, earning money, but I thought that I'd like to try to further my education. I asked my mother if I could go to university, but she said that my father would never allow it. We went through the same upheaval that we had when I had left primary school.

As expected, my father was against the idea. Some fathers would have been proud of a child who was offered a place at university, but my father interpreted it as a rejection of his way of life. No one in my family had attended university since my paternal great-great-grandfather, who was a lawyer and the illegitimate son of a baronet. As I was only seventeen, I required my parents' permission. My father refused to sign his name on the required document and so my mother forged his signature.

I was offered places at Glasgow, Edinburgh and Manchester universities. I decided that the time had come for me to leave home. I wanted my life to be interesting. I wanted to take chances, to be adventurous. I chose to go to Edinburgh University, which meant not only moving out of home, but also leaving everything that was familiar. At the age of seventeen, I left family dramas behind me for the big, wide world of academia. The idea scared me, but excited me too.

I had only ever visited Edinburgh once before, when I was very small, when my family and I flew from Renfrew Airport to Edinburgh for a day trip. I arrived in Edinburgh in 1967, with nowhere to stay and no idea even where the university was. A naïve seventeen-year-old, I suddenly had to deal with landlords, bills and budgeting, as well as finding my way around in a strange environment. Scotland's capital city was very different from my home town of Renfrew. I grew to love the city of Edinburgh in the three years that I lived there. I loved its grandeur and its history. Geographically Edinburgh is about fifty miles from Renfrew, but to me it felt like the other side of the world. My parents did not have a telephone or a car and so there was little communication.

In 1968, when I was eighteen, my sister asked my parents to move to Bermuda, where she was living. My parents were fifty years old and it was a big step for them. My mother had already visited Bermuda, but my father had never been there. It took a lot of courage for them to make that move. My brother, by this time, was living in South Africa, having been offered a contract there as a professional soccer player. My parents moved to Bermuda and from then on I was the only member of my immediate family residing in the United Kingdom. I spent the summer of 1968 working as a chambermaid on the Isle of Wight. I attended Britain's first ever three-day rock festival there and mingled with crowds of excited young people watching Arthur Brown, Tyrannosaurus Rex and Jefferson Airplane.

In many ways the late 1960s was a wonderful time to be young. It was a time of hope, optimism and social change. We joined the Campaign for Nuclear Disarmament (CND) and raised money for OXFAM. We enjoyed many live concerts, Jimi Hendrix, John Mayall & the Bluesbreakers, Bob Dylan, The Incredible String Band, Pink Floyd, Cream.

Adoption and Loss

We read Tolkien, Kerouac, Steinbeck, Lawrence Durrell and Dostoevsky and dreamed of travelling and meeting interesting people. The Women's Movement was beginning to have an impact; more women were entering the workforce and an increasing number of women were employed in senior positions.

Shortly after arriving in Edinburgh, I had met Marie, a student Nursery Nurse (Child Care Worker) from Middlesbrough, in the north of England and shared accommodation with her for most of the time that I lived there. When I returned to Edinburgh from the Isle of Wight, we rented a small one-bedroomed flat. It had a little gas fire in the living room, but no heating in the bedroom. In winter we slept wearing hats and scarves and woke up to ice on the windows - on the inside as well as the outside. Edinburgh is a very cold city in the winter.

We had no television, only a little transistor radio and Marie's treasured record player. We decorated the walls of our flat with articles from the *International Times* and *Oz* magazine. We didn't have beds, only mattresses on the floor.

My mother invited me to spend Christmas of 1968 in Bermuda with them. As I flew across the Atlantic towards Bermuda, the captain announced, *We are now beginning our descent to Bermuda*. I was astounded and thought that he must have made a mistake, as there was absolutely no sign of land. When I did finally spot Bermuda it looked too small even to land an aeroplane on. In fact it is only one and a half miles wide at its widest point.

I fell in love with Bermuda the first time I saw it and it still holds a very special place in my heart. My first impression of Bermuda was that it was the most beautiful place that I could have imagined and had the cleanest, clearest, warmest, bluest ocean water of anywhere in the world, with no pollution. I had no idea before I visited Bermuda that there was such a thing as pink sand. Bermuda has some beautiful pink beaches. The sand is coloured by the coral reef which surrounds the island. The climate is almost perfect; not too hot in summer and not too cold in winter. The air is clean, the beaches are clean and the flowers are glorious. It is truly a lovely place to live. I have visited Bermuda several times over the years and I am always happy to be there.

In Bermuda, my father was a sales representative with an office supplies company. His knowledge of typewriters was very useful in those days. My mother was the matron of a nursing home and they lived on the premises. I spent a few weeks helping Mum with the residents and then returned to Edinburgh in the New Year to continue my studies. I had no idea what the future held, but I had decided to get an education and had hopes for a productive and happy life. Little did I know that ahead of me lay disappointment and distress.

Chapter 3 ... in which Evelyn falls in love

This was a time when sex education didn't exist, either at home or at school and the expectation was that people did not have sexual relationships unless they were married. As a teenager, my plan was to do just that, to wait until I was married before I had a sexual relationship.

There was a young man that I'd had a crush on for a long time. He was friends with some people that I knew and so our paths crossed occasionally. At the end of 1967, we were both invited to the same party and we actually met and hit it off right away.

Over the next eighteen months, we conducted a relationship, which was a combination of friendship and romance. We lived some distance apart, but we visited, wrote letters, exchanged gifts and grew very fond of each other. He travelled to the Isle of Wight in 1968 and spent some time with me there. Early in 1969, he decided to do what many young people were doing at that time, travel around Europe, hitch-hiking, looking for work, exploring. He wrote me long, descriptive letters telling me of his adventures and how much he missed me. He wrote me simple, romantic poems (*The wind blows, The grass grows, And the world knows, This love never ends*.). I longed for his return.

At this stage in my life I had been living independently of my parents for nearly two years, but I had never smoked, never drunk alcohol and never had sex. In many ways I was still quite innocent and idealistic.

When he returned from his travels, he asked if he could move in with me. I was thrilled to think that we would be living together as a couple, which I assumed was a prelude to marriage. I enthusiastically agreed and, on the basis of this arrangement, I agreed to have sex with him. After a few blissful days together, during which he made enquiries about jobs in our area, he said that he needed to go back to his mother's home to collect the rest of his belongings.

He never came back.

The fact that he walked out on me, without a word of explanation, within a few days of our first sexual experience together, was devastating. I felt emotionally bruised and battered, shocked, discarded, saddened and confused all at once. He showed no inclination to discuss our relationship and appeared instead to have suddenly resumed a previous relationship. It was not only a private humiliation, but also a public one as many of our friends knew of our plans and it was very embarrassing to be so casually thrown aside. My self-esteem was at rock bottom. I felt worthless and unwanted. The worst thing was that I realised that I had trusted him and obviously misjudged him. I blamed myself for that. I felt naive and stupid and thought that I should have known better. At the time, I was too sad to be angry. Anger came later.

I had fallen in love and my dreams had been shattered by disappointment and heartbreak. In the aftermath I drifted aimlessly, as if I was living in a bad dream. That dream quickly became a nightmare.

I went to stay with my parents in Bermuda on a two-month working holiday to get away from it all and nurse my broken heart. Not only was my heart broken, but also my spirit. Only with maturity did I come to understand that I had had a lucky escape. I am grateful that he showed me his true character (or rather lack of it) before I committed any more of my time and energy to our relationship.

While I was in Bermuda, I had a date with a handsome young man who appeared to be gentle and caring. I was vulnerable and found myself disarmed by his flattery. Even though I told him that I didn't want to have sex with him, the evening concluded with an uncomfortable sexual experience which, in today's social climate, would be considered non-consensual.

It was all over very quickly. I was so naive and inexperienced that I wasn't even sure afterwards whether or not the sex act had actually been completed. I just knew that I wanted to get away from him. All I could think of while this was going on was that I had got it wrong again, that I was obviously very stupid and still a very poor judge of character. Afterwards he didn't even take me home. He drove me to where I could get a taxi, with the excuse that he didn't have enough petrol. I felt used yet again.

I could never have imagined the enormous impact that brief encounter was going to have on my life.

I was angry and disillusioned, with him, with my first lover and with myself. I not only felt used, I felt soiled and spoiled. I didn't talk to anyone about it. I thought that perhaps if I didn't speak about it that I could pretend that it had never happened. I went home in a taxi, had a shower and hoped that I would never see him again. I didn't.

Back in Edinburgh, four weeks later, I discovered that I was pregnant.

To say that I was shocked and distressed does not even come close to describing my reaction to the news. I was devastated. I received the results of my pregnancy test from the doctor at the Student Health Service, who was very unsympathetic and world-weary. After giving me the news that my pregnancy test was positive (I didn't even understand what he meant, were they positive that I was pregnant or positive that I wasn't?), he dismissed me to 'go away and think about it' and come back in a few weeks.

I left the surgery in tears, wandered the streets, literally not knowing where I was going. Finally, exhausted from my wandering, I found myself by a telephone box and rang Marie, who was at work, awaiting the news. She was the first person I told. Then I found my way home and sobbed alone, for hours, out of sheer misery. I blamed both of my sex partners for the pregnancy, but most of all I blamed myself for having been taken in and used by both of them. I was horrified at the thought that a child had been created by that sordid, unpleasant experience. I was nineteen years old and had just completed the second year of my degree.

A young woman who was unmarried and pregnant in 1969 with no prospect of a hasty marriage was considered to be 'in trouble'. That was me, well and truly in trouble.

Abortion became legal in Scotland in 1967. Doctors could only approve the termination of a pregnancy, however, if there were medical grounds. I asked my doctor if I could get an abortion. He told me that he could only approve an abortion if my health was at risk. I told him that I felt as if I was going crazy. He frowned, sighed with contempt and said, *There is no medical reason why you should not continue with this pregnancy.* I asked for a second opinion. He sent me to another doctor who said exactly the same thing. I had heard of illegal abortions, but I had no idea how to make enquiries about such a thing. I also had no money at all to pay for it. I was too afraid to do anything risky in case it would harm my baby.

It looked as if I was going to have to go ahead with my pregnancy. Although the sexual revolution was beginning to change attitudes to relationships, there was still very little social support – and a great deal of condemnation - for 'unmarried mothers'.

Chapter 4 … in which Evelyn announces her news

I wrote to my mother to give her the news. My mother wrote back asking what was I going to do about it. Her question confirmed for me that from her point of view, it was my responsibility to make a plan. I suspected that my father was not surprised that I was pregnant. I think he considered my pregnancy to be another sign of my rebellious and independent nature, which he had always found difficult to accept.

It was ironic that people had thought that I might 'go off the rails' because I moved away from home at the age of seventeen, yet I actually became pregnant while I was living (temporarily) with my parents. The time came when I felt that I had to announce my pregnancy to the world in general. I have a few memories of breaking the news to people, of their reactions, which were mostly confusion and embarrassment. No one congratulated me. My close friends were accepting and supportive and treated me with sensitivity and compassion. Some commiserated. Some of them asked me about my child's father, but I refused to discuss his identity. As a result of my reticence, they were left to speculate.

At the age of thirteen, I had been invited by some school friends to attend a church social. From there, I became more and more involved with their church and found it to be a caring, friendly environment. I became very committed to the church and remained involved until, in my early thirties, I realised that I was an atheist. Since that time, I have continued to be firmly convinced that all religions are nothing more than elaborate superstitions. However, Christianity did play a significant role in my life for a period of time.

When I told the church leaders about my (in their minds) very unfortunate condition, they presented what they thought was the perfect solution to my dilemma. Their recommendation was that I could atone for my sins by allowing the church to arrange for a married couple, who were devoted and upright members of the church (unlike me, obviously) to adopt my child, who could then be raised to be an obedient and compliant church member. Clearly there were people who deserved to have a child while I certainly did not.

I felt so guilty about having become pregnant, that I allowed myself to be convinced by their proposal. Although it was presented as being the best outcome for everyone involved, I was very aware that this 'solution' was also a way of punishing me for my 'sin'. Losing my child was to be my penance.

I was very vulnerable to their persuasion at this point, because I blamed myself for consenting to sex the first time and I felt that my pregnancy was an indirect result of that decision on my part, even though I had not consented to the sex that had actually led to the pregnancy. I did not describe what had happened as a rape. At that time rape was generally defined as an experience which included violence or the threat of violence. Church members said that they were disappointed in me and that I had let them down; that I had let myself down.

I had to decide what I was going to do about my studies. Would I try to finish university, or just give up? Would I take some time off and come back afterwards? Some people thought that I should leave university and go to live with my parents. I didn't even consider that. Although my father was three thousand miles away, I could feel his disapproval emanating from across the ocean. I certainly didn't want to live with it on a daily basis. I thought about Mr Mackay, my primary school headmaster and his hopes for me to 'make something of myself' and I decided that I couldn't give up, just because of this complication. I felt that at least I could do something to be proud of and finish my degree. I did, however, withdraw from the two extra subjects in which I had enrolled. Those would have given me a better qualification, but I felt that I would do well if I could just complete the bare minimum of subjects in order to graduate.

There were, throughout my pregnancy and the subsequent adoption process, many hurts and insults. There were people who moralised, who judged and who turned away from me. As soon as my pregnancy became known, I was regarded by many, suddenly, as a second-class human being. Some people just looked away when they saw me coming and didn't speak. The most painful situation I had to cope with was the number of people who, although they had known me for many years, now made assumptions about me, simply because I was pregnant. They assumed that because I had become pregnant, I must be promiscuous and probably had been for a long time.

People even asked me if this was my first pregnancy. I was also shocked to be asked if I knew who the baby's father was. I not only knew who his father was, I knew the exact date that he was conceived. Considering this occurred on what was virtually my second sexual experience, it was not difficult to calculate.

One church member, on hearing the news, asked me, *What have you done to yourself now?* At that time, the sexual behaviour of women was judged very differently from the sexual behaviour of men. Sadly, these attitudes still prevail to a large extent. In the eyes of many people, being pregnant was my fault entirely. I had 'got myself into trouble'. I was very hurt that some people regarded me quite differently, as soon as they became aware that I was pregnant.

The Hidden Grief

It seemed that nothing else that I had done was relevant any more. Everything was overshadowed by the fact that I was single and pregnant. Some people avoided me as if my wickedness might be contagious. I suddenly became defined by my reproductive condition. Their attitudes added to my hurt.

I was angry at the people who looked down on me and sometimes I was even angry at the people who were trying to help, because I felt that nothing they could do could make matters any better, although deep down I did appreciate their kindness. Some friends remained loyal and loving and I still appreciate that. In spite of anything they could do, however, I felt as if this was the death of my hopes and plans for the future.

In my early teenage years I had come to understand that people did not always have children by choice. At that age I was suddenly able to make sense of what my father had told me - that he only ever wanted two children. I was his third (and last). I understood then, that I was a 'mistake', the result of an unplanned pregnancy. My father had also told me that when my mother announced that she was pregnant with me, his response had been a resounding, *Oh, no!* He followed that, apparently with, *Well at least it won't be too bad if it's a boy.* It was me. I was afraid that if I kept my child, my anger at my pregnancy and with my child's father would lead me to make my child feel unwelcome also and so I began to think that he deserved better than that and that there would be people who would not have my feelings of anger and would be able to make him welcome in their life. Adoption was beginning to look like the only way to fulfil the obligation I felt I had towards my unplanned child.

I recall my first visit to the maternity hospital. I saw a sign, which read, *All unmarried women must see the almoner* (the name by which a hospital social worker was known in the United Kingdom). I realised, with a shock, that this referred to me. So cowed and apologetic was I, that I didn't even consider not obeying this instruction. I made an appointment to see the hospital

67

almoner and told her that a church was arranging an adoption. In those days private adoptions were still legal. I remember the almoner as prim, middle-aged and distant. I resented what I perceived as her attempts to intrude. I didn't want to answer any of her questions. I felt that it was not her business. I thought that I had no choice but to submit myself to her cross-examination, but I complied as little as possible. I resigned myself to the fact that she was only doing her job. Her job, as I saw it, was to help to arrange the adoption. I never thought of her as a support person and I never considered confiding in her. As far as I was concerned she was never on my side.

When she asked about my child's father, however, I lied. I lied to her for two reasons. First of all, I was too embarrassed to tell her how I had become pregnant. I still blamed myself. At that time young women were expected to be in control of men's sexual behaviour as well as their own. 'Nice girls' said 'No'. What did 'nice boys' do, I wondered. Secondly, I lied because I had been feeling so used and so powerless for so long that it was my one little opportunity to exercise my control. I invented a mythical boyfriend who loved me deeply. He was a student, but just not ready for commitment. I lied to try to make my situation seem a little more respectable. After that first visit, I don't think I saw the almoner again until after my child was born, but the lies and the secrets had started already.

I never felt that the child that I was carrying was *my* child. It was, in the beginning, *his* child. I did not believe that I could ever come to love *his* child because I hated *him*. Once the adoption had been arranged, from being *his* child, my unborn child was then transformed into *their* child. Many years later I read Joss Shawyer's book, *Death by Adoption*, which she wrote in 1979, in which a woman who has been separated from her child by adoption says that she didn't sign away *her* baby, because by the time the adoption took place, the baby was no longer hers; her baby had 'died' already. That was how I felt.

The Hidden Grief

I thought that I was being sensible and responsible by putting my child's welfare first. I only discovered later that it was all a trick. It reminded me of witch trials when women suspected of being witches were thrown over a waterfall in a barrel. If they survived, then that proved that they were actually witches and they were then burned at the stake. If they didn't survive, then that proved that they were innocent - but dead, of course.

In my case, people told me that if I loved my baby I would give him away to a better life. Then after he was adopted some people said that that proved that I didn't really love him after all, because if I had loved him I could never have parted with him. I, along with thousands of other unmarried mothers at the time, was caught in what came to be known as a *Catch-22* situation.

Chapter 5 ... in which Evelyn thinks things over

Adoption seemed the reasonable, logical answer, but I knew in my heart that it wasn't right. It wasn't the way it should be. My fear of raising a child that I couldn't love unconditionally, coupled with my childhood memories of not feeling welcomed by my father, kept me to my plan. To this day my initial, brief reaction to the news of a pregnancy is a sinking feeling in my stomach. The nightmare of my first pregnancy, I know, will never leave me. I felt very let down by life. I felt betrayed. I thought that my dreams and hopes for the future had been shattered. My plans to 'make something of myself' seemed to be in tatters.

Somewhere deep inside me, I knew from the moment that my pregnancy was confirmed, that my life would never be the same again.

My feelings towards my pregnancy and my feelings towards my child were always quite separate. I hated the fact that I was pregnant. I was furious that this unwanted obligation had been forced upon me. I hated my child's father. I hated my first lover for making love to me and then abandoning me. I hated myself, because I believed that I had been gullible and stupid and was therefore responsible for all my problems. But I never, at any time, hated my unborn child.

The Hidden Grief

I felt no emotion for the little stranger who was growing inside me. I did not think that I had any love to offer to this little intruder. I felt only obligation. I was very aware that this innocent child was totally dependent on me for his welfare and I was very protective of him. I was very conscientious about medical matters in order not to disadvantage him in any way. I made sure that I took my vitamins regularly and attended for medical check-ups when required. In fact, after I had shocked everyone with the announcement of my pregnancy, I dropped my rebellious attitude and adopted one of compliance and apology. I felt guilty and responsible and believed that all I could do was to try somehow to compensate for what I perceived to be my mistakes and errors of judgment. I believed that I had created this problem and that I had to be the one who sorted it out.

I also resented everyone else in the world who didn't have this responsibility that had been thrust upon me like a thunderbolt out of the blue. It was all so unfair. My anger simmered all through my pregnancy. Looking back, I realise that there were times when I took out this anger on those close to me. I wasn't angry with them, but with myself and my situation.

I have few memories of being pregnant. I think this is because I spent much of the time in denial, pretending that it wasn't happening. I felt defeated, as if I couldn't win. Life seemed to be conspiring against me. I did consider suicide. Again, I was afraid of not succeeding and harming my unborn child. I thought that I had ruined my life and I hoped that I would die in childbirth. Death seemed like the only escape from this impossible dilemma.

I felt that I was in a no-win situation. I was afraid to keep my child as I didn't want him to be raised to feel that he was a 'mistake', as I was (in 1969, I didn't know of anyone who deliberately had a child out of wedlock and so being illegitimate made it clear that a child was unplanned) and I was afraid to go through with the adoption as I didn't know how I could live with myself afterwards.

Adoption and Loss

My biggest fear was that if I kept him, I wouldn't be able to love him; that every time I looked at him I would be reminded of how he came to be. I felt that he deserved to be loved and I didn't think that I could give him what he deserved. But I also had the fear that if I did go ahead with the adoption, I would hate myself, and worse, that my child would hate me.

At the beginning of my third year at university, Marie and I were still living in our miserable little flat, two flights up in a very old tenement building in St Leonards Street (later the site of the Divisional Police Headquarters). We had no bathroom (only the kitchen sink) and shared a toilet with the neighbours. I had no idea how I could provide for a child. I was told by other students who were studying social work and psychology (and learning about Bowlby's 'Attachment Theory') that children born to unmarried mothers were automatically placed on the 'children at risk' register and that if I took my baby home from the hospital, I would be visited by social workers. They would consider our flat an unfit location in which to raise a child and they would take the baby into state care. They advised me to let the church arrange an adoption for the child ahead of time, rather than let the social workers take him and move him from one set of foster parents to another and maybe never find anyone to adopt him.

I lived on a student grant, which kept me just below the poverty line. I had to work in the Christmas and summer holidays to keep my head above water. My grant was reduced because my parents were both working. The government expected my parents to contribute something towards supporting me, but they didn't. I was in my third year of university and had no idea if, or when, I would find employment, or even what kind of work I might do. I had an Arts degree, but I had chosen subjects which interested me, rather than subjects which might lead to employment. People said afterwards how well I had done to complete my degree. What I remember most about my final year is walking through Edinburgh with my head down, worried and troubled. I thought about my pregnancy all the time. All of a sudden life had become very serious for this nineteen-year-old university student.

There were some unmarried women at that time who kept their children and managed somehow, but they were few and far between. Some of those mothers were in love with their child's father and hoped that he would change his mind and marry them once the child was born, or at least provide financial support. In some cases, the parents of unmarried mothers were willing to support them and their children. My mother told me that I could keep my baby and live with my parents. I asked her what my father had to say about that. She refused to answer. I knew without asking what my father thought. I knew that he didn't want *me* living with them, never mind an illegitimate grandchild.

This was confirmed for me some months after my child was born, when I did find myself living with my parents, briefly. My father told me then, quite unequivocally, that he did not want me there. I could imagine the 'welcome' I would have received with a bastard child in tow. I could not bring myself to grovel and beg from my father. I felt that he would have made my life a misery with his resentment and I feared that he would have made my child's life a misery too. If he had found himself supporting my child and me, he would have been angry and resentful. Throughout my childhood, my father had almost managed to convince me that I was worthless. The fact that I was pregnant seemed to prove that he had been right. I couldn't let him treat my child the same way.

People said that I could have other children, as if that would make up for it. They said that I could put it behind me and meet a nice boy who would marry me so that I could make a fresh start. The implication was that I would be able to forget about my child and have a happy life without him.

At that time, to my knowledge, there was no regular government payment to unmarried mothers. I had been raised under the good, old, Protestant work ethic, that if you had a child, you had to support your child. There was very little in the way of childcare provision in the late 1960s. There was little demand for childcare as very few mothers of children under school age were in the workforce.

The childcare that was available was provided only for children who were considered 'at risk'. Children in childcare were often viewed as disadvantaged and abandoned. I was told by professionals that children who spent their days with strangers did not bond and so would probably grow up to be psychotic at worst, delinquent at best. I was told that it would be cruel of me to keep my child and then force him to endure the daily deprivations of childcare.

Others convinced me that keeping my child would be selfish, that I had to put his interests first. At that time, there was no question that being at home with a full-time mother was the ideal situation for a young child. I thought that allowing him to be adopted would protect him from growing up with the stigma of illegitimacy. I didn't realise at the time that he could grow up with the stigma of being adopted instead.

Chapter 6 ... in which Evelyn waits

Having made a commitment to the church, that they could deliver my child to the adopters they had chosen, I endured the remainder of my pregnancy with a combination of resignation and fear. I deliberately suppressed any emotions that I may have developed as my child grew inside me as I was afraid of how difficult it was going to be to do finally what I felt had to be done. I tried to shut down my feelings and carry on with my life, even though it was growing more and more difficult to climb the two flights of stairs to our little flat. Looking back, I have no idea how I would have coped without Marie. She understood me and cared for me and never let me down. I will be forever grateful to her for her unfailing support and sympathy.

I visited my paternal grandmother (my last remaining grandparent) just before Christmas. I was very fond of her and visited her as often as I could. I felt very guilty not telling her that I was carrying her great-grandchild. She was eighty-seven years old and I thought that it would upset her and so it was easier to keep quiet about it. I was very concerned that I wouldn't be able to visit her again until after I had had the baby, as I knew that I couldn't conceal my pregnancy much longer. I was worried that if I didn't see her for a long time she would think that I didn't care about her. As it happened, she died two months later. My aunt wrote me a letter, which said, *We buried your Gran last Friday.* I was very upset that no one had told me that she had died in time for me to attend the funeral.

At that time, student grants were paid three times per year, in a lump sum at the beginning of each term. This made it very difficult to budget. Christmas was approaching and not only was I pregnant, but I had no home to go to and no family to share the festive season with me. I was pregnant and it was going to be the first Christmas I had ever spent without my family, as they were all overseas.

Marie's parents kindly welcomed me into their home for Christmas, although they didn't know about my pregnancy. I spent the whole time I was there hiding my rounded tummy. Marie and I tried not to smile when her mother said that she thought I was looking thinner. Marie's friends teased me about my expanding girth with the words of a popular song, '... you're gonna carry that weight, carry that weight a long time.' Little did we know for how long I was going to carry the 'weight' of that pregnancy.

Christmas was the end of the first term and grants would not be paid until the second term started towards the end of January. Fortunately, I had been able to get a job for a few weeks before Christmas in the sorting office of the General Post Office in Edinburgh. Part of my duties was collecting the letters which children had posted to Santa and putting them in the rubbish bin, which made me feel a bit guilty, but it was helpful to have a little extra money around the festive season.

A few memories stand out from my final year at university in Edinburgh. I contracted chickenpox while I was pregnant, which was rather embarrassing at the age of twenty. I also had a very bad bout of gastro-enteritis. I didn't eat for two weeks. Marie tried to feed me coddled eggs. I had three doctors who attended me at home, but they all said that there was nothing they could do. The third doctor who came felt my abdomen and then asked me if my periods were regular. I told her that I was five months pregnant. Perhaps she thought that I hadn't noticed.

The Hidden Grief

As the pregnancy progressed, it was difficult to find suitable clothing. I had no money to invest in a maternity wardrobe and I was trying to hide my pregnancy from as many people as possible, to avoid having to answer upsetting questions. Someone kindly gave me a piece of blue material. From this, I made myself a large pinafore. I sewed every seam by hand, trimming the neckline with bias binding and I wore it almost until it fell apart.

Marie made me a beautiful grey cape, which I wore all through the cold Edinburgh winter. It was a severe winter, with lots of snow and ice. I was afraid often of slipping and falling, for fear it would hurt the baby. I remember walking slowly along side streets, holding on to garden fences, hand over hand.

I have a vivid memory of being in the Cafe Royal (a popular haunt of Edinburgh students) with a good friend when I was about seven months pregnant. He asked me about my plans for the future. I told him that the baby was to be adopted and I wept. He asked me why I was so sad about the idea of my child being adopted. I told him that my biggest fear was that if I went through with the adoption plan that my child would hate me.

He then told me that he was adopted and that being adopted was fine. He didn't hate his original mother (some years later, thankfully, he was able to tell her that in person). That cheered me somewhat. I felt that he had turned out to be a really nice person and so maybe being adopted wasn't so bad after all.

I tried to prepare myself to deliver *their* child, although I actually had no idea how to prepare myself. Nothing in my previous experience had equipped me to deal with this situation.

I had no medical preparation at all, as unmarried women were not allowed to attend antenatal classes (when I had to attend the hospital for check-ups they always called my name out as Mrs Burns, which felt very strange because 'Mrs Burns' was my mother, not me).

My doctor continued to treat me with contempt and so I did not have the confidence to ask him any questions about the forthcoming event. I had no knowledge of the mechanics of childbirth, but I had an idea that it would be painful.

I kept my feelings very much to myself throughout my pregnancy. I believe that I was afraid to allow any feelings to surface for fear that they would overwhelm me. Looking back I see myself like an emotional jack-in-the-box, with the lid held down tightly. In spite of the support of some close friends, I felt totally isolated in my experience.

I remember often lying in bed at night, alone, weeping, with the loneliness and enormity of it all. I suppose my mourning had already begun, even before my child was born. I was mourning my lost innocence, my lost lover, my lost hopes and dreams, as well as the future loss of my child. Even then, I worried about the effect on my unborn child of my deep sorrow.

The last vivid memory I have before I went into labour was of an incident that occurred three weeks before my child was born. I had sneaked into Mothercare, a large store in the centre of Edinburgh which sold baby and child products. I felt as if I had no right to be there, because I wasn't a genuine expectant mother, as I wasn't wearing a wedding ring. I kept my left hand in my pocket so that no one would notice. I felt as if I was not a legitimate mother-to-be, because I actually was not going to be a mother after the baby was born and I felt that if anyone found me out they would ask me to leave. I realise that these feelings may seem quite illogical, but pregnancy is not a time for logical thinking; it's a time of deep emotions.

These feelings were also connected to the feeling that it was not my baby I was carrying. In spite of this, as the time to give birth drew closer, I had been fantasising about actually being able to care for my child. In Mothercare I looked longingly at the clothes and toys and imagined myself buying them, like the other expectant mothers who were there.

I left the shop, feeling very dejected and was waiting at a bus stop in Princes Street, when I met a friend called Keith. He asked me where I was going and chided me for taking the bus. He persuaded me to walk with him up the Mound (a steep hill in the centre of Edinburgh). It was a sunny, spring day in April and he was cheerful and energetic. At the top of the Mound I was breathless, but persevering. I mentioned something about the difficulties of climbing hills in an advanced state of pregnancy and discovered that he didn't know that I was pregnant. I believe that he was the only person who ever congratulated me on hearing that I was pregnant. At the time I contradicted him. Now I feel immense gratitude towards him.

At that time I couldn't see that there was anything to be celebrated; the whole business seemed to me to be destined to end in misery – for me, at least. This warm, generous man told me that whenever a child comes into the world, there is joy. I think that was my first clue that I could love my child. However, by that stage I felt obligated to follow through with the adoption plan and that to consider any other outcome was just being fanciful.

I had felt that I had to make a decision early in my pregnancy. It seemed too difficult to have to tell people that I was pregnant without being able to add immediately that I was going to 'do the right thing' and have the baby adopted. As I had clearly been irresponsible in allowing myself to become pregnant, I felt that I had to convince people that I was now being responsible and making sensible plans. To admit that I had no idea what I was going to do with regard to my baby would have made them think that I was totally feckless.

Because I had made a commitment to allow my child to be adopted, I tried to suppress my feelings and not allow an emotional relationship with him to develop. I should have waited and allowed nature to take its course. If I had, I would have been more in tune with my feelings after my son was born and perhaps I would have known that I could love him.

My mother decided to come to Scotland for a visit and she was with us in Edinburgh at the time of my son's birth. I remember going to the airport to meet her. I hadn't seen her for nearly a year. I only ever saw my mother cry twice in her life. The first time was when her own mother died. The second was when she saw me in an advanced state of pregnancy, in Edinburgh.

My baby was due on the 15th of May. I knew that the baby would come very close to that date because I knew exactly when he was conceived (looking back, I think he may have been conceived on the weekend that the Woodstock Festival took place, but I wasn't feeling particularly full of peace, love and music at the time). He was born at 13.13 on Saturday the 16th of May, 1970. The time of his birth appears on his birth certificate. This has always been the practice in Scotland.

On the afternoon of Friday, May 15th, I was in the university lecture theatre watching 'Gimme Shelter' a documentary about the Rolling Stones. I felt pains in my stomach and started to watch the clock. I turned to Marie and said that I was having pains every fifteen minutes. She asked did I want to go home. No fear, I wanted to see the end of the film! We went home afterwards and timed my pains for several more hours. There was not a lot of progress, but the pains continued. At 11.45 pm we rang for a taxi and my mother accompanied me to the hospital.

I was separated from her as soon as we entered the hospital. The rule was that only husbands were allowed in the maternity unit. If you didn't have a husband, too bad, you were not allowed a substitute. My mother sat in the waiting room until 6.00 am, but they refused to let her see me. It was a large hospital and she had no idea where to find me. I was bathed (I had to kneel, not sit) and put in a bed in a dark room with the curtains round my bed. There was no nurse in the room and no doctor visited me.

There were other beds, which held other women, in various stages of labour. During the night some of them were taken out, screaming and crying in pain. I had no way of summoning assistance. At one point during the night I needed to go to the toilet and I called out several times. There was no one there; no one heard me. I got out of bed and tried to find the toilet, but couldn't. No one visited me, no one spoke to me, no one checked to see if I was all right. I was terrified and alone.

{The only hospital that I know of to have issued an apology for the way unmarried mothers were mistreated in the past is the Royal Brisbane and Women's Hospital, in Queensland, Australia. They issued an apology in 2009 which was commemorated with a plaque in 2018.}

I lay awake all night and then found myself next morning in the delivery room. My mother, by this time, had given up and gone home. Strangely, I have no memory of pain during the birth itself. I have no idea if I was drugged, as the hospital refused to allow me access to my medical records when I requested them years later. My labour seemed to be very slow and I believe that I was given something to hurry things along.

I remember being asked whether or not I had practised my breathing exercises. To explain why I didn't know anything about breathing exercises all I had to say was, *I'm not married*. That explained everything. Everyone knew that if you weren't married you weren't allowed to go to antenatal classes.

Chapter 7 ... in which Evelyn's baby is born

Looking back, I feel as if I somehow detached myself from the experience of giving birth to my first child. It seemed that childbirth happened not to me, but in spite of me. I believe that's why I can't remember the pain. I remember that there was a moment of panic; that there were calls for a doctor. I was afraid - of course I was afraid. I had no idea what was happening and the medical staff seemed to take charge of everything and deliberately exclude me from the proceedings. I have no idea whether they treated me that way because I was unmarried or if they treated every woman like that.

The doctor arrived and my baby was delivered with the help of forceps. I discovered afterwards that his shoulders had become stuck in the birth canal. I learned that if I had gone into labour when I was alone (as some young, frightened women did) and had not obtained medical assistance, the baby and I would both have died; the child first and then me. Anecdotal evidence suggests that birth difficulties are common in cases where babies are to be adopted. It's as if the mothers somehow try to hold on to them for as long as possible.

Someone told me that I had a son. I was surprised. I was surprised that I had a baby at all. In spite of having had nine months to get used to the idea, I still found it hard to believe that

The Hidden Grief

all this was really happening to me. The midwife handed my baby to me when he was born and I held him. I don't know if that was done deliberately or if they didn't realise that he was to be adopted, but I will be forever grateful that it happened. We gazed at each other for a few moments, my little man and I. When I looked at him, my immediate feeling was one of enormous pride. I was amazed that I had produced this living thing; that this brand new little person had come out of me. I realised there and then, in that split second when I saw him and held him, that he was a whole new person who had nothing to do with betrayal, rape or anger. He was fresh, new and mine.

Looking back, I realise that, in that moment, I knew that I could love him after all. But it was too late - too late to change my mind. His prospective adoptive parents were anxiously awaiting him. I had promised them my child and I felt that I couldn't go back on my word. Hadn't I thought it all out and hadn't I realised that it was for the best? Just seeing him didn't change any of that, didn't change the facts - the facts that I had no job, no husband, no money and not even a decent place to stay. I felt that I had nothing to offer him except my love, but I couldn't see how love could feed and clothe him. Yes, I did love him then, but I felt that it would be selfish and irresponsible of me to keep him.

After the birth my son was taken from me. I was placed in a large ward with about forty beds, each with a new mother and each with a new baby beside the bed, twenty-four hours a day. That was the hospital policy. There was a baby by every bed except mine, that is. All day and all night I heard babies crying, watched mothers tend to them, hold them, kiss them and feed them. I wasn't even allowed to draw the curtains around my bed and be alone with my pain, except at rest time in the afternoons.

Every day I watched happy husbands and grandparents visit all those other mothers, bringing them flowers and gifts, cooing and laughing and discussing family features and similarities. I remember one friend did bring me flowers to the hospital. I was angry with her, although I realise now that she meant well. I felt that flowers were for celebration. For me, this was a tragedy. I didn't feel that flowers were appropriate.

For those other mothers there were lots of hugs and kisses, lots of smiles. It seemed such a cruel punishment to have to watch everyone else's joy when I was suffering so much. Some people who noticed that I didn't have a baby with me, whispered and looked disapproving. Others looked as if they felt sorry for me. I certainly felt very sorry for myself. Every night I spent in the hospital I cried myself to sleep and had awful nightmares.

When my milk started to come in I was very surprised. I hadn't been warned that this would happen. I thought you only made milk if you started to breast-feed. My breasts were bound tightly. It was very painful.

I felt so very sorry for my son, because he wasn't being welcomed into the world the way all those other babies were and I felt sorry for myself too, because I wasn't being accepted as a mother. I trusted the people who were going to adopt him to welcome him, to give him the hugs and kisses that he wasn't getting in the hospital. I trusted them to give him the unconditional love and acceptance that children should receive from their parents. Looking back, I realise how naive I was to assume that because a child was adopted, all this would necessarily follow.

The social worker at the hospital had told me that I had to give my son a name. I had mixed feelings about that. It seemed pointless, as I knew that his name would be changed when he was adopted. I thought that it was an empty gesture on their part to acknowledge me as his mother briefly, but then take my motherhood from me for the rest of my life.

They told me to forget about him and 'get on with my life'. I only discovered many years later that it's not forgetting our lost children that allows us to get on with our lives, but remembering them.

84

The Hidden Grief

Mum and Marie asked if they could go to the nursery to see my son. They told me that he was beautiful. Mum said that his ears were like my father's. I had mixed feelings about spending time with my baby. In one way I wanted to see him. I was very drawn to him and desperately wanted to hold him, but I was afraid of how painful it would be. I thought that the more time I spent with him the harder it would be to part with him and at this stage in the proceedings, I didn't think that I had any choice but to do just that.

A few days after the birth, however, I knew that I wanted to see my son, no matter what. I didn't ask permission; I was afraid that they would refuse. I anxiously wandered through the corridors until I found the nursery. I asked the nurse if I could look at him. She was very kind and said that I could hold him if I wanted to and told me about his feeds and his progress.

I sat with him in my arms for a little while. I looked at his tiny fingers and unwrapped him to see his tiny toes. I pressed my face against his ever-so-soft cheek and kissed his smooth forehead. I whispered in his little ear, *I love you. I will always love you and you will always be welcome in my life.*

Then the doctor arrived with a group of students. He was very angry that I had been allowed to see my son and shouted at the nurse and at me, very rudely. He told me that if I 'didn't want him' I should just 'leave him alone'. He was scornful and hurtful and I could see the students lower their heads with embarrassment. I wanted to kick him and shout back at him, but I felt powerless. I held on to my baby until he had left the room, however and only then did I creep back to bed. Although I was pathetically compliant throughout the whole process, I had still a little spark of rebellion left in me. He gave orders that no one was to see my baby after that and when my mother tried to see him again the next day, she was turned away. For years afterwards I used to mutter darkly whenever I thought of that doctor, *He'll be the first to go when the revolution comes.*

Chapter 8 ... in which Evelyn's baby is taken away

Many adoptions at this time were arranged by churches. Churches *knew*, as did many health professionals such as doctors, social workers and psychologists, that children of unmarried mothers would most likely grow up to be juvenile delinquents and that single women could not give children the stability they needed to become productive, stable adults.

When my son was six days old I was told that the representative of the church, who had arranged the adoption, was coming with his wife to collect my baby from the hospital the following day. The next day came and I cried and sobbed for hours. I can still hear myself saying over and over, *They're taking him away today, they're taking him away today.* A gentle, Irish nurse came and sat with me and held my hand. She told me that if she were in my position she would do the same thing. That reinforced for me that I was indeed 'doing the right thing'. Finally the doctor decided to sedate me because I was disturbing the other mothers.

I waited for the couple who were collecting my son (who knew me personally) to come to speak to me, to offer me some words of comfort, perhaps reassure me that I was doing what was best for my child, that he would go to a good home. No one came near. I waited and waited and finally I decided that I would try to see my son one more time, to say goodbye, before they took him from me. I went back to the nursery and looked around. My baby was gone. They had taken him without even telling me. I felt that I must be beneath their contempt, that they couldn't lower themselves to visit me. I also felt that I was totally insignificant, that they only wanted my child, but didn't want to become involved with me as a person, or my feelings. I wanted to be acknowledged as my son's mother. After all, I was still legally his mother at that time. Perhaps they were afraid that if they talked to me about the adoption, I might change my mind. It seemed that my child had to be taken surreptitiously, that it couldn't be done openly.

It was as if everyone was conspiring to pretend that it wasn't happening. Whatever the reason, I felt very hurt and insulted. No one from the church ever brought up the subject of my child again.

Once my son was gone I desperately wanted to get out of the hospital. I kept asking when I could go home. The doctor visited me the following day and told me that as I had developed a post-natal uterine infection, I would have to stay in hospital for a few more days. I had what used to be called 'childbed fever'. Left untreated, it can be fatal. I told him that I couldn't stay any longer as my final exams started the next day. He told me that I could go home that day, but that I would be putting my health at risk. I didn't care about my health. It was of no importance to me. I just wanted to get out of there. I hadn't lied, my exams did start the following day. I had to 'sign myself out of hospital' to ensure that the hospital would not be held responsible if my condition deteriorated.

I remember leaving the hospital. It was as if I was looking at the world through glass; as if I was not really present and not really interacting. I felt detached from my physical body and quite drained of any emotion. Two days after I was released from hospital, my mother and I went to the Registry Office in George

Adoption and Loss

Square to register the birth. At the Registry Office I was asked, 'Are you married to your baby's father?', then, 'Is the baby's father here to have his name recorded on the birth certificate?', then, 'Are you keeping your baby or is he to be adopted?' After answering all of those embarrassing questions in a very public place, I watched as the word 'Adopted' was written carefully on the bottom of his birth certificate. Even then, I remember thinking that it hadn't actually happened yet and how dare they do that.

The day after I left the hospital I was at the university for an exam. I went into the cafeteria and one of the women working there noticed that I had obviously had my baby.

'What did you have?' she cooed.

'A boy.'

'And did you manage to get him into child care?'

'Yes.'

There began the lies. Already I was denying my experience. I couldn't bring myself to try to explain to her what had really happened. I decided that I would never see her again and so I would not have to keep up the pretence. I never set foot in the cafeteria again. I wanted to be away from the university and away from Edinburgh, but I couldn't leave until after my exams.

The next few weeks passed in a blur. Mum left and everyone else went on with their lives, as if it was all over. I sat my final exams. I felt numb and empty. I felt drained of all feeling. I was wounded to the very depths of my being. I felt as if my life was over. I spent a lot of time in Greyfriars Churchyard, among the dead. I felt dead inside and wished that I was lying among them. Finally I was notified that I had passed my final exams. I couldn't bring myself to attend my graduation ceremony.

I couldn't face all those smiling, confident students, optimistic about the future. Besides, no one from my family was going to be there in the audience to applaud me. I have gained two post-graduate qualifications since then, but I have never attended a graduation ceremony.

The Hidden Grief

I was very restless and unhappy. I felt as if I was living in a fog. I had no idea what I wanted to do or where I wanted to be.

I spent a couple of months travelling around Europe, sleeping under trees, on beaches and occasionally in youth hostels. It was a relief to be with people who knew nothing about me. Returning to Edinburgh, I had no idea what to do next. Before making any other plans, I had to sign the consent form for my son to be adopted. I have only a vague memory of this event. In my mind and in my heart he already did not belong to me and so the actual signing of the form was almost a technicality. I left Edinburgh in September, 1970 and have never lived there since.

Chapter 9 ... in which Evelyn moves to Bermuda

The only place I could think of to go next was Bermuda, where my parents were living. When I arrived, they were living in a small, one-bedroomed flat attached to a large home of which my mother was housekeeper. They had no room for me and it wasn't my home, but I had no home, no money and no idea where else to go. My mother made me welcome, of course. My father said, bluntly, *I don't want you here.* I was determined to find a job and move into my own accommodation as soon as I could.

I had been desperate to get out of Edinburgh, where my child was born, to escape from the memories and now I found myself back in Bermuda, where he had been conceived. I made enquiries and found out that the father of my child had left Bermuda just after I did. I was relieved that I would not run the risk of seeing him.

Those early weeks in Bermuda were very difficult. On the one hand it was a kind of fresh start and good for me to be away from where I had been so miserable, but, on the other hand, I knew no one except my immediate family members and I was very sad and lonely. I didn't want to be there, but then I didn't really want to be anywhere at that particular time. I spent six weeks living with my parents.

The Hidden Grief

I had no work experience to speak of and, although I had a degree, I wasn't actually qualified to do anything. I contacted the Department of Education and asked about teaching positions. I applied for other jobs too, but with no success. Then one Friday I received a call from the headmaster of the Berkeley Institute, inviting me to meet with him the following Monday to discuss the possibility of employment as a teacher of French. They were in desperate need of a French teacher and they offered me the job. Learning to be a teacher on the job was hard work and there were times when I wanted to give it up, but I had no money to go anywhere else and so I persevered.

Once I had secured a job, I moved out and rented a flat. My plan was to get on my feet financially and then leave. I had no idea where I would go, but I didn't feel at all welcome or at home in Bermuda. Within six months I had saved some money, but I decided that I should stay until the end of the school year, as I didn't want to let the school down. By the end of my first year there I was thoroughly enjoying the work and starting to feel more at home. After four years there I loved Bermuda, the school, the staff and the students and it was a great wrench to leave.

I did make friends in Bermuda and many of them are still friends to this day. None of them knew about my son, of course. My deception continued and became more entrenched. The more time passes, the more deeply buried the secret becomes and the harder it is to think of revealing it. While I was living in Bermuda, I made lots of visits to New York, to Boston and back to Scotland. In New York I wandered around Greenwich Village, soaking up the atmosphere, buying books and jewellery. On one trip I paid a taxi driver to drive me from one end of McDougall Street to the other so that I could say that I had driven past Bob Dylan's house. I had no idea which one it was and so I drove past all of them just to be sure. In Boston I walked through the grounds of Harvard University, just so that I could say, 'I went through Harvard (in the front gate and out the back).'

Adoption and Loss

During this time I took up yoga, which I found very beneficial. Yoga has been a part of my life since then and I am grateful to the wonderful yoga teacher who first taught me in Bermuda in the early 1970s. In one class we performed a meditation in which we were required to focus on an apple. We closed our eyes, relaxed and imagined our apple, its smell, its colour and its texture. We took our apple on a trip from when it grew on the tree to when it came into our possession. I was amazed at how my meditation took on a life of its own, seemingly outwith my control. My apple was beautiful, healthy, shiny and colourful as it grew on the tree.

Eventually I bought it, in a paper bag, from a fruit shop. As I walked down the street I thought about eating my apple and looked forward to the pleasure it would give me. I drew it from the bag and held it in front of my face to admire it for a moment first. All I could see was a large, ugly bruise. It didn't take much for me to work out that that was how I felt about myself. Like my apple, I might appear at first glance to be healthy and appealing, but on closer inspection I would be found to be ugly and unappetising.

For many years I worked very hard not to let anyone get close enough to find out. Years later I discovered that not only many original mothers, but also many adopted people felt themselves to be imperfect and second-rate.

Not long after the loss of my son I began to have frightening dreams, nightmares perhaps.

They were of two types, dreams of exposure and dreams of separation. In the dreams of exposure I would find myself having a shower or sitting on the toilet when all of a sudden I would realise that I was in the middle of a department store or on a busy street, with everyone looking at me. I would panic and feel very exposed and want to hide myself. In the dreams of separation I would be on a bus or a train with a baby and then I would get off without thinking and leave the baby behind. As I watched the vehicle speed off into the distance with my baby, I would realise, too late, that I had been careless and had let my baby go. I felt guilty and worthless. Many other original mothers have since talked to me about their dreams. Often they dream about hearing a baby crying and trying desperately, in vain, to locate it. My dreams haunted me for many years.

While I was in Bermuda I thought of my child every day. I looked at other babies and wondered if he was sitting up yet, if he was walking, talking, what he looked like. I carried the picture of his little face with me in my mind and held on to it tenaciously. It was the one thing that no one could take from me. I also took up a voluntary position, teaching young women who had left school early because of a pregnancy. As I worked with these young women, I envied them so much because they were raising their children. I wanted to do all that I could to support them.

I also was instrumental in persuading my headmaster to change the school policy on young women having to leave school if they became pregnant. The school did not have a written policy, but whenever a student announced that she was pregnant, the assumption was that she would leave school as soon as possible.

One of my most promising students became pregnant at the age of fourteen. Her mother contacted me and I visited them at home to talk about her future at the school. I encouraged her to stay on at school for as long as possible. She was extremely brave and continued with her studies.

The headmaster called me into his office and asked if it was not time she should be leaving school. I told him that I saw no reason why she should leave; she was in perfectly good health and an excellent student. I persuaded him to see the logic in my argument and she continued at school as long as she felt comfortable there.

After that I visited her every weekend and passed on work from her teachers so that she didn't get behind with her studies. She had excellent family support and was able to complete her education and soon had a beautiful home and a prominent position in the workforce. She remains a good friend and I am privileged to be her daughter's godmother.

Having got it so wrong, ie been pregnant without being married, I really wanted to get it right. I got married, in Bermuda, three years after losing my son. I had only known my husband for three months when we married. Just as well my Grandmother wasn't still around or she would have been muttering, *Marry in haste, repent at your leisure.*

I told my husband before we were married that I had had a son and he accepted that, but he never mentioned it again. My husband had also lost a child through adoption and so I felt that he would understand my pain.

When I was suffering and missing my son over the years, however, I was never able to share that pain with my husband. Fortunately, we managed later to build a relationship with the daughter from whom he had been separated by adoption and she and I still keep in touch.

We decided that we wanted to have a child as soon as possible after we were married. I became pregnant five months into the marriage. We were delighted. I thought that this time I had got it right. I had a loving husband and I was expecting a child that was planned and wanted. I happily announced my pregnancy to friends and family. When I was about three months pregnant, however, I realised that my husband's behaviour had become bizarre and frightening. In later years I pondered whether this was a result of his own adoption loss issues coming to the surface in anticipation of the birth of our child.

I begged him to seek professional help. He flatly refused and would not accept that there was any problem. As his behaviour became more alarming, I began to feel that I had made a big mistake, that I could never be happy with him, that I had misjudged yet another man.

I only learned several years later that he was suffering from a serious personality disorder. Perhaps if he had agreed to address this disorder early in our marriage, things could have turned out differently.

I became very depressed, as I felt trapped. After what I had gone through in my first pregnancy I did not feel that I could leave my husband and go through another pregnancy alone. After thinking that I had got my life back on track and had made a positive move, I now felt that I had gone from one disaster to another. After having gone through the difficulty of announcing my first pregnancy to everyone and having to deal with their disapproval and now having told everyone that I was pregnant again, I couldn't bring myself to announce that my marriage was over, after less than a year. I was struggling to convince myself that I wasn't a total failure in life. I decided to battle on and conceal my unhappiness.

While I was pregnant, my husband decided that he wanted to live in Scotland, in spite of the fact that he had been born and raised in Bermuda and all of his family was there. In 1974, I found myself back in Renfrew, with just a suitcase of clothes to my name, married, pregnant and making yet another fresh start.

Chapter 10 ... in which Evelyn returns to Renfrew

Having my second child, the first child of my marriage, was a confusing time for me. It was important for the hospital to know whether or not this was my first child because there were different arrangements for first time mothers. When it came to caring for a child, feeding, bathing, handling, it was my first child, but physically, of course, it was my second.

Every time I was asked the question, it hurt. I couldn't pretend to medical people that I hadn't already had a child as there were physical signs that I had, but I wanted to make it clear that I knew nothing about looking after babies, because I desperately wanted to know everything there was to know about caring for a baby, as I felt that I needed to be the best mother possible to this child.

I was delighted to be able to have another child and felt that life had given me a second chance. However I was so afraid that something would go wrong. I felt that I really didn't deserve to have a child and I refused to look ahead to bringing my child home from hospital, as I couldn't quite believe that that was going to happen. I thought that someone would find me out, realise that I had 'given away' a child and decide that I wasn't fit to have another one. I couldn't even bring myself to buy anything for my baby before I went into hospital.

The Hidden Grief

There was only one thing I had prepared for him. I had spent many hours crocheting a large, round, white, woollen shawl to wrap him in, as he was born in the middle of a severe Scottish winter. Before he was born my husband cut it to pieces in a fit of temper. I hadn't the heart to start another.

When I was in labour, my baby's heart stopped beating. I wasn't surprised. I thought, *This is it, I knew I'd never be allowed to have this baby to keep.* He survived that, only to develop jaundice. I found myself, yet again, the only mother in the ward without a baby by her bed, as he was in the special baby unit for several days. I was bereft. I thought everyone must know that I wasn't like other mothers. When I went to the unit to feed him, I couldn't wake him. I sat and held him and cried, convinced that he was going to die.

Then they said that I could go home, but that my son would have to stay in hospital for further treatment. I became very upset and refused to go. There was no way I was going to walk out of a maternity hospital again with no baby. **I was convinced that if I left him there I would never see him again.**

I have a very clear memory of actually bringing him home from the hospital. I carried him up the pathway to the house, treading carefully on the frozen, sparkling, white snow and just as I reached the door I looked over my shoulder, convinced that this was too good to be true and that someone was going to step forward and say, *Where do you think you're going with that baby?* I faced the same dilemma with the birth of each subsequent child, when answering the question, *How many children do you have?*, but it was more poignant with the first. I read book after book on child and baby care. I felt that I had to prove myself - to prove that I was worthy to have the care of these children.

I thought that if I had lots of children that I would somehow fill the empty space left by the loss of my first child. I had four children in the space of five years. They filled my time, if not the empty space left by their brother.

Adoption and Loss

In their early years, I devoted myself totally to my children. None of my children ever had a bottle feed; they were all completely breast-fed. Through two of my pregnancies I breast-fed until I was five months pregnant. None of my children ever ate prepared baby foods. I cooked everything for them myself. I always used cloth nappies, never disposable ones. No one was going to be able to say that I wasn't a good mother.

Although I endured domestic abuse in my seven years of marriage, I also had four children. All of my children were planned and wanted and I was very grateful for them. They have brought me much joy. I chose to be a full time mother to them when they were very young. I left the paid workforce when I was pregnant with the first of my four children and did not return to work until my youngest child started school. I never regretted that decision. I believe that my children benefited much more from the time that I spent with them than they would have from any increase in our standard of living. The ten years that I spent out of paid employment were a wonderful investment in my children's lives.

There were good times in my marriage, but my husband was so unpredictable that I could never relax with him, even when things seemed to be going well for a while.

People have asked me why I stayed married for so long. There were several reasons. I was afraid of yet another failure. My self-esteem was low. I felt that I had to give marriage every possible chance and only gave up when I was absolutely sure that there was nothing more that I could do to save the situation. Because I felt so guilty about my first son, I agonised over how to do what was best for my other four children. Ending a marriage is never a decision to be taken lightly, especially when there are children.

I desperately wanted my marriage to be a success and did finally manage to persuade my husband to attend marriage guidance counselling with me. We attended one counselling

The Hidden Grief

session during which he gave the answers that he thought a good husband should give. Even though he didn't tell the truth, the counsellor said at the end of the session, *Do you really think this marriage is worth saving?* What might she have said if she had known how bad things really were, I wondered.

To other people, my husband was charming and affable and many people had difficulty believing that, in the privacy of our home, he was a vindictive, abusive husband.

He did finally see a psychiatrist after we separated and she told me that if I reconciled with him, he would make my life a misery to punish me and that, in fact, my life would be at risk. My husband had already threatened me on several occasions. I knew already that I had no intention of going back. When I separated from my husband the eldest of my four children had just turned five and the youngest was five weeks old. Shortly after our separation, he returned to Bermuda. He did come back to Renfrew some months after our separation to try to persuade me to give the marriage one more try. His method of persuasion included breaking my jaw. I immediately filed for divorce. He returned to Bermuda and never supported or contacted his children from then on.

I believe that my previous experiences with men, coupled with my sadness and low self-esteem related to the loss of my first child, meant that I did not have the courage to confront the problems in my relationship with my husband very early in the marriage, when they first arose. If I had done so, much suffering could have been avoided. It seems to me ironic now that I was encouraged to give up my right to raise my first child because I thought that he deserved two dedicated parents and yet I ended up raising my other four children alone. I remained single until all of my children were living independently.

After the divorce, the children and I stayed in the same little flat for two years. It was a two-bedroomed upstairs flat, hardly big enough for the five of us, especially on rainy days and there are lots of those in Renfrew. When my husband was there the children had all slept in one bedroom, but, after he left, I moved out of my bedroom and slept in my sleeping bag on the lounge room floor for two years, so that the children could have the bedrooms. Every day, in winter and often in summer too, I carried buckets of coal upstairs to light the fire to keep us warm. In winter, I often had first of all to take a kettle of boiling water down to pour over the lock on the coal bunker, to melt the snow, so that I could open it. I didn't have a car and walked most places, with or without the children. Money was very short and we were grateful for cast-offs from friends and neighbours. Although all the members of my immediate family were in Australia by this time, I did have aunts, uncles and cousins who were wonderful and very supportive. I also had many great friends, who visited frequently and kept my spirits up. Raising four children by myself has not been easy, but we are still a close, happy family.

Chapter 11 ... in which Evelyn moves to Australia

Two years after my marriage broke up, I emigrated to South Australia with my four children. My parents and my brother and sister were all living there by this stage and I wanted my children to grow up within their extended family.

When I was eighteen, my parents had left Scotland to live in Bermuda. After I went to live in Bermuda, they had returned to Scotland. After I returned to Scotland they moved to Australia. When I finally arrived in Australia, I told them that they were getting too old to run away from me any more; they might as well just stay put now. They lived out their days in Australia and I was happy to be able to spend time with them and help them as they aged.

Our journey from Scotland to Australia was exhausting and lasted forty hours. I had four children under the age of seven and in the whole forty hours there was no time when they were all asleep at the same time. This meant, of course, that I got almost no sleep. One suffered from travel sickness and vomited at regular intervals, one had German measles (although we didn't know what was wrong with her until we arrived) and they were all restless for most of the time.

Arriving in South Australia, coming back to my parents, reminded me of arriving in Bermuda. It was the same familiar pattern. Mum welcomed us, while Dad frowned. The children and I had to stay with my parents until I could find a suitable place for us to live. My parents were living in a small, two-bedroomed, upstairs flat and, of course, they had no room for me, not to mention four children as well. My aunt was staying with my parents on holiday at the time and so my parents had one bedroom, the four children and I had the other and my aunt slept in the lounge room. My father did not tolerate the children well and so the five of us spent most of our time in the bedroom to avoid him. Happily, this only lasted for a few weeks and I was able to rent a house, to everyone's relief.

Here I was making yet another fresh start, with only a few suitcases full of clothes and the children's favourite toys. While I was living in Scotland, I was in fear of seeing my child somewhere. I knew that if I saw him I would want him. I used to read newspaper reports of tragedies or accidents involving children, or, worse still, of children being abused and wonder if that was my child who had suffered.

In one way it was hard to leave my son behind in Scotland and travel to Australia, but in another way it meant that I no longer had to worry over harrowing media reports involving children. Over the years I never forgot my first son. I thought about him constantly. Anyone who has not lost a child through adoption may find it hard to believe that I thought about him so much, but those who know will understand. I felt ashamed, guilty, sad, unworthy and frightened. I kept my feelings to myself and never talked about him. My other four children didn't know about him and my family members, who did know, never mentioned him.

My first son was born on my brother's birthday and so every year when we were celebrating my brother's birthday, I was wishing I could be celebrating my son's birthday too. When the whole family was singing 'Happy Birthday To You', inside I was screaming in frustration, *It's my son's birthday too, you know!*, but

102

The Hidden Grief

I didn't let my feelings show. I desperately wanted some acknowledgement of my first child, but I didn't expect anyone to understand and so I cried alone, just as I had done when I was pregnant. Every Christmas I was wishing that I could buy him a Christmas present. Every Mother's Day I was wondering if he would ever acknowledge me as his mother. I thought all the time about whether or not I would ever see him again.

By the time I arrived in Australia, I had been lying and denying my son for twelve years. It didn't get any easier. I felt guilty and embarrassed about it all the time. A simple question such as, *How many children do you have?* caused me extreme discomfort. I hated lying all the time. I was afraid to tell anyone the truth, however, as I thought that people would never understand. I couldn't understand myself how it had happened. How could I expect to be able to explain it to anyone else? Besides, I hadn't been able to bring myself to tell my other four children and so I couldn't tell anyone else until the children knew.

All those years, I was in a constant state of anxiety, terrified that someone else would tell my children before I felt ready. All in all, I put myself under a lot of pressure by keeping my child a secret. It felt like a millstone around my neck. I felt like an impostor. I knew that my new friends did not really know me. They only thought they knew me. I was constantly afraid of being exposed for what I really was - a woman who had 'given away' her child. I thought that if people really knew me, they wouldn't like me. I cried many more lonely tears.

I knew that under Scottish law, my son would have access to his original birth certificate when he was seventeen years old. In May 1986, when he was sixteen, I took the first step towards contacting him. I wrote to New Register House in Edinburgh to check if there had been any changes to the adoption law.

They forwarded my letter to Birthlink in Edinburgh, who advised me that they had placed my name on their contact register.

103

Adoption and Loss

They also told me that under Scottish law there was nothing that I could do except put my name on the register, then wait and hope.

In 1988, because of the review of the Adoption Act in South Australia, there were articles in the local newspapers about adoption. I read about an organisation called Jigsaw, which helped family members separated by adoption. I rang them. They referred me to a support group specifically for mothers who had lost children through adoption.

The group was called ARMS, which at that time stood for the Australian Relinquishing Mothers Society. The name was later changed to the Association Representing Mothers Separated from their children by adoption, although the acronym remained the same. ARMS in South Australia was formed in 1982 and was successful in persuading the state government to make changes to the Adoption Act, which would allow adults who had been adopted as children and their original mothers equal rights to access identifying information about each other when the adopted child had attained adulthood.

In 1989, after the ground-breaking Adoption Act was passed, ARMS received government funding, which allowed them to employ staff. The first social worker employed by ARMS was my late friend, counsellor and colleague, Meg Hale, who, in 2014, published a history of ARMS, called *Mothers in ARMS*. In her book, Meg explains how ARMS in South Australia was formed, as well as ARMS groups in other states, after the Third National Adoption Conference in Adelaide. She also outlines the impact of the South Australian group, not only on the members, but on adoption legislation and practice.

For many years I experienced a sense of belonging at ARMS, as I shared experiences with other mothers and enjoyed their friendship and support. When I joined ARMS I realised at last that I was not alone in my adoption separation experience and was finally able to share my feelings with other women who understood them. I was able to have counselling to help me to understand how and why I lost my child. Through the counselling I learned to channel my anger at the loss of my child into productive activities and to appreciate that my loss will always be with me.

Groups like ARMS can provide a very supportive and healing environment for their members, as well as fulfilling an important role in educating the general public and lobbying for changes in legislation and policy.

As far as I am aware, the ARMS group in South Australia was the only one in the country to receive funding which allowed them to employ staff. For a group of volunteers, without professional guidance of any kind, to run an organisation which involves employing staff is a major challenge. In the case of ARMS, the volunteers in question are people who have been wounded by their experiences and so there is always the danger that a toxic and destructive work environment can develop. Sadly, this is what I experienced when I was employed for four years as the ARMS Counsellor/Co-ordinator, a position from which I made the difficult decision to resign in 2003.

After attending my first ARMS support group meeting, I decided that the time had come to break my silence and talk about my lost child. My first step was to tell my other four children that they had a brother. I couldn't live with the fear and guilt any longer. I had no idea how they would react, but I decided that nothing could be worse than spending the rest of my life in fear of having my shameful secret exposed. They were aged nine, ten, thirteen and fourteen. I sat them down and said that I had something important to talk to them about.

My fourteen-year-old said, *It's not the birds and the bees is it, Mum?*

Not quite, I replied.

My thirteen-year-old then surprised me by saying, *You're not going to tell us that we're all adopted, are you?*

No, I said, *but you're getting warm.*

105

Adoption and Loss

When I did manage to tell them that I had another child, they were stunned. There was a lot of anger, there were many tears and accusations and there was little sympathy. My ten-year-old said, *Well, where is he then?* I think she thought that he was going to appear through the doorway the way people did on the television programme, *This Is Your Life.* When I said that I didn't know where he was, what his name was or even if he was alive or dead, they were even more upset. They said that he was part of our family and belonged with us and how could I have given him away?

I tried to explain how different attitudes were all those years ago and how everyone then thought that it was the right thing to do. It was difficult for the children to imagine what it was like when I was a teenager, as society had changed so much since that time. I tried to explain that in my teenage years there was a terrible shame attached to being pregnant and unmarried, that it was an embarrassment and a disgrace. I told them that there was tremendous pressure on unmarried mothers to give their children to married couples, because it was believed to be in the child's best interests.

I explained that there was also social pressure on married couples to produce children, which created a demand for babies from infertile couples. Because in their lifetime unmarried motherhood was no longer such a disgraceful state, it was hard for my children to understand the pressure that had existed then.

They were very upset that I had deceived them and felt that they couldn't trust me and that perhaps I had kept other things from them. They thought that I should have told them when they were younger, as it would have been easier for them to accept then. My problem was, of course, that when they were younger, I was not ready to tell other people about my first son. I couldn't tell my children and then ask them to keep it a secret. I couldn't tell the children until I was ready to tell everyone. They were also angry that I hadn't been able to locate him.

The Hidden Grief

I told them that I had been trying to find him and that I hoped that one day he would be part of our family. My nine-year-old's response to that was, *He'll probably hate you because you dumped him when he was a baby and never want to see you again. Have you thought of that?*

I told her that I had thought of little else for nineteen years. She went on to say that it made her very sad to think that he might not want to meet me again, because, *If he never wants to meet you again, he'll never know what a great mum you really are.*

The children were desperate to find their brother and got very angry when I told them that, under Scottish law, we weren't allowed to know anything about him. They complained about how unfair it was that they couldn't contact their own brother.

Telling my other children was not easy, but it was a huge relief and a very welcome release from the tyranny of deceit. I felt like someone who had been released from prison after serving a long sentence. I was finally able to be my true self after years of pretending to be otherwise. I had always encouraged my children to express their feelings honestly and so I had to accept their reactions to my news. Years later the children told me how sorry they were that I had faced all of that sadness alone for so long before feeling ready to share it with them. I am proud of them for understanding and accepting my experience.

Although my name was already on the contact register, I wrote to Scotland again to ask if there was anything else that I could do. They told me that there was no way that I could get access to any information under Scottish law and that, as my name was on the contact register, there was nothing more that I could do - just wait and hope.

Chapter 12 … in which Evelyn tries to find her son

I visited Scotland in 1989 and before I left Australia, I was able to obtain a copy of my son's original birth certificate, which was wonderful. The word *Adopted* written on the bottom was like a knife through my heart. However, I felt that it belonged with me and I was very glad to have it. I had also contacted a representative in Scotland of the church which had arranged the adoption, to tell them that I was going to be visiting Scotland and to ask if there was any chance of meeting my son, who was then nineteen years old, when I was there.

The church representative was actually very helpful and contacted my son's adoptive parents to explain that I would be visiting Scotland for a short time and that I probably would not be able to visit again for some years. His adoptive parents became very angry at what they viewed as an intrusion and refused to consider my request or to tell my son about it.

I enjoyed my holiday in Scotland and after I returned to Australia, a friend sent me a newspaper cutting about an adoption agency in Glasgow. At first I didn't think that they could help me because they hadn't arranged the adoption of my child. I thought that because it was a private adoption, none of the adoption agencies would know anything about it. However, I decided that it couldn't do any harm to ask them and so I wrote to them in 1990, just to ask if there was anything else that I could do to search for my son, apart from having my name on the contact register. I received a reply in December 1990 and got a huge shock. The adoption counsellor had obtained my son's adoption records and had rung his adoptive parents. I felt that she should have discussed this with me first and asked me how I wanted to proceed. I felt marginalised and disempowered.

She didn't know, of course, because she hadn't felt it appropriate to consult me, that the church had already approached his adoptive parents and received a very angry reception. They were not pleased at being approached yet again and, in spite of the fact that my son had not lived at home with them for some time, again refused to discuss the matter with him, even though he was legally an adult.

The adoption counsellor did tell me that my son's first name was Stephen. It was wonderful to know his name at last. The counsellor also said that his adoptive mother had described him as 'a fine boy' and said that he was at university. The counsellor told me that according to Scottish adoption law, '... an adoption agency may provide such access to its case records and disclose such information in its possession as it thinks fit for the purpose of carrying out its function as an adoption agency.' That is obviously very ambiguous and apparently the various adoption agencies each interpret the law in their own way. I hadn't realised that an adoption agency could access adoption records for adoptions in which they had not been involved.

I wrote again, in desperation, to ask if there wasn't anything at all that I could do and I received a letter dated 26th February 1991. The adoption counsellor told me that their agency had made the decision not to try to contact adopted people directly on behalf of original parents until they reached the age of twenty-five.

Even then, she said, they do not have search facilities and rely on the goodwill of the adoptive parents to inform them of the adopted person's whereabouts. She said that my son's adoptive parents refused to tell him that I was trying to find him, as they 'knew' without asking him that he wasn't interested in having any contact with me.

The counsellor told me that I could write to her again when my son was twenty-five, but that there was no guarantee, of course, that his adoptive parents would be any more co-operative then. The news was heart-breaking. All I had ever wanted was to give my son the opportunity to choose whether or not to have contact with me.

I became very despondent, disappointed and discouraged. I felt that I had been so close, but had been prevented from taking that final step. All I could do was wait and hope that he had heard my whispered message when I held him in the hospital all those years before.

As it turned out, I didn't have to wait very long. I received another letter from the same adoption counsellor dated 19th March 1991 saying, 'On Wednesday 13th March a young man came to my office inquiring about his birth parents. It was Stephen.'

I was astonished and delighted. My first thought was that his adoptive parents had had a change of heart and decided to tell him that I was searching for him, but I was wrong. The letter went on to say, 'He did not know that I had approached his mother and father.' It seemed that he had heard me when I had spoken to him all those years before in the hospital nursery after all.

It was a wonderful feeling to know that he had taken the initiative to try to find me. I was delirious with happiness. I felt that I had gone from the depths of despair to the heights of elation within the space of two weeks. The counsellor went on to say that she did not give him my address, as she did not have my permission to do so and suggested that I either write a letter which she would pass on to him, or let her know if I wished him to write to me directly.

The Hidden Grief

I sent her a fax asking her to give him my address and telephone number and to invite him to call me and reverse the charges as soon as possible. He rang as soon as he heard from her. It still amazes me that a week after I received her letter, which gave me no hope at all, he was in her office with the news that I had hoped for all those years, that he wanted to contact me. I shudder when I think of how hit and miss the whole process is and how easily that contact might not have been made.

For many years I have written to politicians in Scotland, begging them to consider legislation such as that which exists in South Australia and which has been operating successfully since 1989, to allow adult family members who have been separated by adoption to manage their own affairs like the adults that they are, but, so far, to no avail.

The telephone call came at about 11.30 one night when I was asleep. Although I had been anxiously awaiting a call from him, I was also afraid that it was all too good to be true and that it wouldn't happen. He didn't reverse the charges and so I suggested that I call him back. I was terrified to let him go in case something would go wrong, but I wrote down his number. When I put the receiver down I was trembling. I couldn't allow any time to collect myself, however, as I was so afraid that he wouldn't be there when I rang back, or that he'd given me the wrong number.

Our telephone conversation lasted two and a half hours. It's a very strange experience to be asking your own child how tall he is, what colour his eyes are, what his hobbies are. I wanted to know everything about him. The first question he asked me was why I had given him up. The second was why I had never tried to find him. I heard the anger in his voice and it cut me to the quick. I panicked and thought maybe he does hate me, maybe he only wants the answers to his questions and then I'll never hear from him again.

Then I explained to him that I wasn't allowed to know anything about him and that I had done all I could to try to find him. I wanted to know first of all if he had been well cared for and had a happy upbringing. I wanted to know where he had lived, where he went to school, what he enjoyed doing, did he have close extended family and did he have a partner. He wanted to know where I was born, why I was in Australia, was I married, did I have other children, who was his father. Finally, two and a half hours later, we decided that we'd said everything we wanted to say for the time being. I was still very scared that this might be our only contact. I so much wanted to know him, to see him, to be able to explain it all to him. We agreed to write to each other and send photographs.

His first letter came and I thought, *He writes beautifully; he hasn't inherited my awful scrawl*. I devoured his words and examined the photographs over and over again, searching for a resemblance. We actually do look alike, but that wasn't clear from the photographs. I just couldn't believe my good fortune. The next step was to arrange a meeting. As I wanted him to meet the other members of my family, there was no point in considering having me go to Scotland and so we began to plan for him to come to Australia.

I had missed him so much over the years, I knew that I wanted nothing more than to meet him again and I was prepared to do whatever it took to make that happen. Also I felt that I had to try to find a way to meet him while he was interested in the idea. I was still afraid that if I didn't 'strike while the iron was hot' that he might change his mind. I booked his flight for a time that suited him and prepared myself for an anxious wait.

Chapter 13 ... in which Evelyn discovers the truth

Stephen came to Australia in September, 1991 and spent three weeks with us. The other four children and I met him at the airport. It must have been a bit daunting for him to arrive and see us all lined up there. Our reunion was not tearful or demonstrative. I was battling to stay calm so as not to embarrass him. He was cool and polite. I introduced him to the other children. Looking back, I think we were both extremely brave and extremely nervous.

I was amazed that he was actually here, living in my own home. It was such a thrill to be able to introduce him to my family and friends, who all made him feel welcome. Even though my immediate family members all knew that I had had a child, no one had mentioned him over the years. I remember taking him to meet my parents. My father stood up (which was rare as he had arthritis in his knees, which restricted his mobility), extended his hand and said, *I'm very pleased to meet you.*

Suddenly, amid my joy, I felt a surge of anger well up inside me. I wanted to say, *Well, you weren't very pleased twenty-one years ago. You weren't prepared to make him welcome then!,* but I kept silent. I had spent so long hiding my feelings that it had become a habit - one that I still find hard to break. I have no idea what my father was thinking as he met Stephen.

Adoption and Loss

Although I had carried the picture in my head of my first sight of my son when he was born, somehow, over the years, I had lost that picture. I was very distressed about that, as it was all I had to hold on to. I tried desperately to remember what he looked like. I felt guilty, as if I had betrayed him by forgetting. When I saw him again, twenty-one years later, my picture of him at birth miraculously came back. It was very welcome.

One of the things that he said about our reunion at the airport was the shock that he got when he saw my next eldest son. He said, *It's the first time in my life that I've seen someone with my face*. I showed him my class photograph, taken in my first year of primary school, in a group of about forty children. He picked me out immediately. He said, *I had the same little face when I was that age*. I couldn't take my eyes off him. I wanted to look at his hands and feet, his ears, his eyes. I wanted to know about everything he had done. I froze when he told me about his emergency appendectomy when he was twelve and how if he hadn't got to the hospital he could have died. If he had died, I would never have known and I would never have known what he had become.

I wanted to watch him eat and sleep. I wanted to hear him talk and watch him walk. As soon as I saw him at the airport I saw how much he looked like me. Afterwards I kept searching for other similarities. Was he musical, did he like languages, what made him laugh? It was interesting that he wore so many earrings as it reminded me that I had had my ears pierced while I was pregnant with him. We talked about his birth. I had tried to obtain copies of my medical records from the maternity hospital. I was told that they had been destroyed. When Stephen asked for copies some years later he was told that he could have them, providing he produced a letter from his doctor. His doctor refused to provide him with a letter.

I think that my son and I are very fortunate that we are similar in many ways and we were able to establish a close

114

The Hidden Grief

relationship without much difficulty. I told him towards the end of his stay here that I had always loved him because he was my son, but it was so wonderful to get to know him and find that I actually liked him too. The relationship between a parent and a child who have been separated since the birth of the child is a unique relationship, unlike any other. It takes patience, understanding and effort on both sides, but the rewards can be immeasurable.

When Stephen was here, a friend asked us what it was like to get together again. I turned to my son and said, *Well, was it good for you?* We both smiled. Fortunately we have a similar sense of humour. The other children coped well with having him here and made him feel part of the family. My younger son was out with him on one occasion and a friend commented, *I didn't know you had another brother.* My younger son replied, *He ran away from home when he was a baby; he's just come back.*

When I tell people the story of our separation and reunion, they often say how they love to hear about a *happy ending.* It is happy at the moment, but it is far from being the end and while it is wonderful to have my son in my life now, his early years are lost to me forever. I didn't see him take his first step, I wasn't there for his first day at school and I didn't see him graduate from university. I haven't forgotten the agony of missing him for twenty-one years, of not knowing if he was alive or dead, of wondering if he hated me. When he left, at the end of his three-week holiday here, it was very difficult. Separating from him again reminded me of my original separation from him and brought back my original pain.

The telephone calls and letters continued. In 1992 he toured the United Kingdom and had a great holiday visiting friends and relatives of mine. Many of them became his friends too. I was delighted that he had made contact with some of the people whose support I had appreciated throughout my pregnancy. He wasn't able to meet Marie until 2002, when he visited her in Toronto. I was so thrilled that these two people who were special to me had become friends. Stephen came back to Australia in August 1996 for a year's working holiday, spending three months with us before travelling around the country.

He has been living in Australia since 2004, apart from some periods of time when he travelled overseas and worked in other countries. After many failed attempts, Stephen was finally granted Australian citizenship in 2012. The Department of Immigration did not recognise our relationship and so he was not able to claim any family connection in Australia.

Although it's wonderful to have him in my life again, as part of my family, I realise that our reunion efforts could so easily have ended in disappointment for both of us. In Scotland they are proud of the fact that they were one of the few countries to have always had what they term *open adoption*. What they mean by this is that adopted people in Scotland have always had access to their original birth certificates when they became adults (originally at the age of seventeen, but now at the age of sixteen). Sadly, however, original parents have no legal right at all to any information about their lost children, although some agencies will act on their behalf to make contact with adopted, adult children. The implication is that original parents cannot be trusted with such information and need 'responsible' people to act for them. I find that assumption insulting.

Gradually I learned about my son's efforts to find me. He was told when he was four years old that he was adopted and had always been curious about his origins. At the age of thirteen he found out by chance that adopted people could get access to their original birth certificates when they were sixteen and he memorised the details of how to go about doing that. He did get his original birth certificate when he was sixteen and went to an adoption counsellor to try to find me.

Although my address was on his birth certificate, the flat that I was living in when he was born had been demolished. I had married overseas and changed my surname. I had then emigrated to Australia and so really he had very little hope of ever finding me. I had no family member who shared my original surname in the Scottish telephone directory and so he had very little to go on. He went back to the counsellor occasionally to see if they could come up with something more, but wasn't getting anywhere.

Finally, in March 1991, he decided to try yet again. He rang the adoption counsellor he had been seeing and made an appointment. The counsellor rang him back and said that he was unable to access his file, because it was at another agency. My son had no idea why that would be, but he went to the agency in question simply to get his file, to take to his own counsellor to continue his search.

He was amazed when he found out that the reason they had his file was because I had been looking for him. He got upset because the counsellor refused to give him my address, as he didn't want to use an intermediary; he wanted to contact me directly.

He asked if she could get him a cup of coffee and while she was out of the room he took the file out of the drawer and copied down my details. He said that he was going to allow her a week. If he hadn't heard back from her in that time, he was going to contact me himself.

Of course, I got back to the counsellor the same day that I got her letter and my son and I were talking on the telephone within a very short space of time. I asked him why he hadn't put his name on the contact register and he said, *What contact register?* In spite of all his efforts to find me, no one had ever told him that a contact register even existed.

If he had not decided to approach his counsellor again exactly at the time his file was with the agency I had contacted, he may never have known that I was searching for him. It was a rather stunning example of synchronicity. I am very proud of him for having the courage and persistence to search for me and not give up.

117

Adoption and Loss

I find it difficult to describe the difference it has made in my life to have all five of my children around me. I don't think that anyone who has not experienced an adoption separation can truly understand the huge impact it has on a person's life. It is not an overstatement to say that my whole life was transformed when my son and I got in touch with each other. That contact put an end once and for all to my fear and ignorance about the person he had become.

For Stephen, it also meant an end to fear and ignorance about the person he was. Now he knows that he was never rejected nor abandoned by me, that I did love him and that I never forgot him. Because I have researched my family history, he also has information about his ancestors going back to the eighth century.

I was even able to tell Stephen that I had lied to the social worker about the identity of his father and that he hadn't, as he had thought, inherited his mathematical ability from his original father.

I don't take anything for granted in our relationship. I have told him that he has no obligation to me and I appreciate that our relationship continues because we both genuinely want it to continue. I accept him and love him for the person that he is.

In the middle of 1998 I travelled to Scotland and was finally able to fulfil my dream of being in Scotland with Stephen and going with him to the places which had been significant to me throughout my life.

We went together to Renfrew and visited the site of the house in which I was born and the site of the Blythswood School (now, sadly, demolished). We also travelled to Edinburgh together and I showed him where I was living when he was born and where I was when I went into labour.

We even went together to the hospital in which he was born and requested access to our hospital records, but were refused. We also walked up The Mound together.

118

The Hidden Grief

All through these experiences I was pinching myself, as I could hardly believe that after all those years I was revisiting those places with my son. It was nothing less than a dream come true. I cannot imagine what my life would be like without him and I hope that I never have to find out.

Chapter 14 ... in which Evelyn contributes

As I complete the revision of this book, in 2018, I have been with my second husband for eleven happy years. My four children from my first marriage and their respective spouses, along with my eight grandchildren, all live within twenty minutes' drive of our home. We enjoy frequent family gatherings.

Marie, who now lives in Canada, is still a dear and cherished friend and has been since we first met in Edinburgh more than fifty years ago.

I have been constantly in touch with Stephen since we reunited twenty-seven years ago and he now has Australian citizenship and currently lives and works in South Australia. We see each other often and he has a good relationship with my other four children.

I can now look back on my earlier life with a kind eye and feel empathy for my younger self. I know that the separation from my first son has affected every area of my life and that my experience of that separation and loss is with me constantly. In spite of that and to some extent because of that, my life has been not only very interesting, but also very fulfilling.

Since I first contacted post adoption support services in the late 1980s, I have been learning about the long term impact of adoption separation and also teaching others. I'm sure that I will continue to learn and to teach, as I maintain my contacts with post-adoption organisations and individuals around the world.

I take great satisfaction from knowing that I have contributed to educating members of the community, as well as professionals, particularly those in the field of social work and psychology, about the long term outcomes for family members separated by adoption. I have also been involved with designing and advancing adoption apologies. I have been active in providing training and education in many different locations to many different audiences about the long term outcomes of adoption separation.

I have also promoted changes in the way that vulnerable children, not only in Australia, but also in other countries, are protected and cared for. For many years I have tried to convince legislators that adoption is not an outcome that is in the best interests of children and that we owe it to them to support more child-centred methods of caring for children who are unable to live safely with their parents.

I have also promoted programmes that educate and support parents so that they can create more positive and therapeutic home environments for their children. Having raised my four children as a single parent, I am very aware of the pressures of parenthood and I believe that providing more assistance and education for parents would allow more children to reside safely in their families of origin.

I have been given many opportunities to be useful by assisting and supporting those who have experienced adoption separation. I am grateful to all those who have invited me into their lives and shared their experiences and emotions with me.

Adoption and Loss

The Hidden Grief

{This paper was presented in Melbourne, Australia in October, 2012 at the 10th Australian Adoption Conference and was subsequently published on-line in the *Australian Journal of Adoption Vol 6, No 1 (2012)*

Sinking the Mother Ship

(Definition: A mother ship is a craft which carries one or more smaller craft; the mother ship may recover the smaller craft or may go its own way after releasing it.)

Introduction

Human beings are mammals. Like other mammals, they are driven by their instincts. One of the strongest of these is their instinct to reproduce, in order to ensure the continuation of their species. Throughout the ages, different human societies have tried to control people's reproductive urges, by creating their own rules about the circumstances under which reproduction is socially acceptable, based on their particular belief systems.

In my book, **Adoption Separation – *Then and now***, I have published a collection of accounts written by forty-five parents who lost their children to adoption, between 1958 and 1989, in Australia, Canada, England, Ireland, New Zealand, Scotland and the United States. I know from my long involvement with the adoption community that their stories are representative of the experiences of many unmarried parents in those countries during that timeframe. This paper, which focusses mainly on the Australian situation, aims to provide a social context for those experiences.

Adoption and Loss

In the middle of the twentieth century, in many English-speaking countries, women who gave birth and were not legally married at the time (unless they had been widowed during their pregnancy), were referred to as 'unmarried mothers'. Not only were they defined by their marital status, they were also defined by what they were not. Their children were labelled 'illegitimate', which meant that they were born outwith the legal protection provided by marriage. The unmarried mothers referred to herein are those who gave birth within the historical and geographical parameters of the book, although mothers in other times and in other places have had similar experiences.

Certain dominant beliefs in those countries were grouped together to form a powerful, dangerous mass, which exerted its influence, to a large extent covertly, operating under the surface of society. When translated into actions, this mass of beliefs led to thousands of illegitimate children being whisked away from unmarried mothers and absorbed, apparently seamlessly, into other families. This became a secret tidal wave of adoptions on which many were swept up and many were swept away.

To those who were not adults during this period in history, in those locations, it may appear that removing many thousands of children from their mothers, on the basis of their marital status, was an act of unmitigated cruelty. However, the behaviour of those who were advising and caring for unmarried mothers was seldom randomly malicious. It was largely based on a set of beliefs, which may now appear indefensible and even, to some, incomprehensible.

Understanding that belief system, however, can provide a context within which to position the experiences of unmarried mothers, at the time when so many of their children were taken from them to be adopted. While this exploration does not in any way excuse what happened to those mothers and their children, it does assist in understanding their experiences, which can play an important role in the healing process.

The Hidden Grief

The Adoption Iceberg

It is well known that icebergs have been responsible for sinking ships. For many unmarried mothers, such as those who contributed to the book, their experience as a 'mother ship' was sabotaged by that powerful, dangerous mass which I have designated the 'adoption iceberg'.

The apparently benign portion of the iceberg which was visible above the surface represents the positive perception of adoption in the general community, as the ideal solution to the 'problem' of an illegitimate child.

Adoption was intended to give the child a home which was emotionally and financially stable and to protect the mother and her family from scorn and disgrace. It was the much larger, invisible mass of the iceberg, lurking beneath the surface, however, which presented the real threat to the mother ship. This was made up of a dangerous combination of beliefs, the potency of which gave the adoption iceberg its enormous power. Many young women who found themselves pregnant and unsupported felt that their mother ships were shipwrecked by this formidable and treacherous configuration.

Beliefs about women

Adoption icebergs existed in societies which held certain beliefs about women. The story of Adam and Eve in the Garden of Eden is the basis of the notion of original sin, which underpins the Christian tradition. Eve, in her role as the first woman, was not only responsible for the fall of Adam, she also bears the enormous responsibility for bringing sin and death into the world, through her weakness and disobedience. According to the Christian bible, if Eve had not acted as she did, the human race could not have come into being. However, Eve became the scapegoat and labour pains were her punishment. This tale set the scene for women being held responsible for men's behaviour and being blamed for enticing men into immoral actions. It also forged a close link in people's minds between sexual behaviour and sin.

The ideal of pure womanhood which formed the basis of the cult of the Virgin Mary was also a powerful theme in the Christian tradition. A great deal of emphasis was placed on the sexual purity of women, although there was rarely the same expectation for men.

Historically, the Christian church has preached vigorously against sex outside of marriage. In eighteenth century Scotland, for example, many unmarried expectant mothers found themselves sitting on the 'fornicators' bench' at the front of the church, for all to see and condemn. The Puritans apparently forced an adulteress to wear a scarlet letter 'A' in a conspicuous position on her clothing, to announce her sin to the community.

Women who had had a sexual relationship outside of the marriage contract were condemned as immoral and sullied. A woman's personal value was closely linked to her sexual behaviour.

Even in the twentieth century, many unmarried expectant mothers internalised these beliefs and felt a sense of personal shame and responsibility, because they had transgressed the ideal of pure womanhood, which was integral to Christianity. Some hid themselves in residential homes, which were usually operated by religious organisations, or moved to a part of the country where they were unknown, to avoid experiencing contempt and disapproval. This isolation rendered them particularly vulnerable.

Many of them were forced to work hard, to impress on them the error of their ways and to discourage them from repeating their 'mistakes'. Some religious workers stressed to mothers that the way to make amends for their sins was to agree to adoption. Unmarried mothers were often told that they did not deserve to be allowed to raise their children. Following in the footsteps of Eve, they were scapegoated.

The Hidden Grief

Sadly, many of these young women found that the Christian emphasis was much more on retribution than on compassion and that some religious personnel were not content for judgment and punishment to be postponed until the afterlife. Unmarried mothers were judged by people who had no authority to pass sentence on them. For many of them, their principal 'sin' was naivety.

So widespread was the belief linking a woman's value to her sexual behaviour, that many unmarried mothers whose children were adopted felt such a sense of shame and guilt that they could not bring themselves to reveal the existence of that child, even to those closest to them. They had failed to live up to the expectation of sexual purity and they feared that they would be judged and found wanting.

Some unmarried mothers avoided revealing the pregnancy to their parents and arranged the adoption themselves, in order to protect their parents from distress and to protect themselves from their parents' disapproval and disappointment. An unmarried woman with a child was considered by many to be 'second-hand goods' and there was a general reluctance on the part of many parents to welcome a woman in this situation as a daughter-in-law.

In other cases, parents who discovered that their unmarried daughter was pregnant made arrangements for their grandchild to be adopted, believing that by doing so they were protecting their daughter, her child and the reputation of the family. Sending their daughter away and concealing the truth about her situation also protected the parents from being confronted on a daily basis by the mother ship (their offending daughter) and the small craft which she was carrying (their illegitimate grandchild). Their fears for their children and grandchildren were not groundless, as the association of what was perceived as sexual sin with personal value was a very strong one in the community in general and not only among those who would have described themselves as religious.

Adoption and Loss

The legal status of illegitimate children was always precarious and they were discriminated against in various ways. The widespread support for adoption was partly based on a general feeling in the community that children should be protected from experiencing the outcomes of their parents' irresponsible behaviour.

Beliefs about families

Beliefs about families were vital to the stability of the adoption iceberg. In the middle of the twentieth century, in the countries represented in *Adoption Separation*, there were still very clear distinctions between married parents and unmarried parents. Women, to a much greater degree than men, were defined by their marital status. A woman who was married, or who had been married and widowed, was referred to as 'Mistress' (commonly shortened to 'Mrs') while a woman who had never been married, no matter how old she was, was referred to as 'Miss'. In correspondence, a married woman was addressed by her husband's first name. A letter to the wife of Mr Robert Smith, for example, would be addressed to 'Mrs Robert Smith'.

These practices were linked to nineteenth century English law, under which a woman's legal identity ceased to exist after marriage. It was not uncommon in Western countries for women born in the early part of the twentieth century to leave the workforce when they were married and never return to it. Being a wife and mother was their career.

The expectation in these societies was that only married people would engage in sexual relationships and that a woman, in particular, would remain 'pure' until her wedding night. Her purity was symbolised by her white wedding gown. At her wedding, the bride was 'given away' by her father to her husband, which symbolised a transfer of ownership and responsibility. Marriage for many women was a transition from obeying their fathers to obeying their husbands.

The Hidden Grief

Although oral contraception (known as 'the pill') was available from the early 1960s, its long term risks were largely unknown and it was viewed by many women and some doctors with trepidation. There were also fears in the community that the contraceptive pill would encourage promiscuity and few doctors in the 1960s could be persuaded to prescribe it for unmarried women. Some doctors, in fact, would only prescribe oral contraception to married women with the permission of their husbands. Abortion was illegal in many places, including parts of Australia, until the 1970s and even then, access was restricted. Many doctors would sanction an abortion only if the mother's health was considered to be seriously threatened by the pregnancy.

It was generally accepted that children who were raised by one parent were less likely to achieve their full potential in life and were more likely to suffer the disadvantages associated with poverty. Most of these children were raised by their mothers and, considering that there were limited employment opportunities for women at this time and that it was legal to pay women less than men for doing the same work, this was not surprising. There was also a fear that if the mother later married, the complications of a step-parenting situation could have a negative impact on the child's well-being.

Beliefs about work ethic

Towns in Britain were traditionally divided up into parishes, each with its own church, which took care of the poor and the needy. Even now, those who obtain assistance from the government are sometimes described as being 'on the parish'. Churches were responsible for welfare until the introduction and gradual development of the welfare state in the twentieth century. Britain has for many years considered itself to be not only a Christian but also a Protestant country, committed to the 'Protestant work ethic', which meant that people were admired for working hard in order to provide for themselves.

This ethos underpinned many societies, regardless of their religious leanings and was carried to Australia, New Zealand and North America by British migrants. A single man had the responsibility of supporting himself and a married man had the responsibility of also supporting his wife and children. Being 'on the parish' therefore, has traditionally been viewed as a shameful and unfortunate condition, if it resulted from people failing to fulfil the social expectation of being independent and able to support themselves.

The belief in the Protestant work ethic formed another important component of the adoption iceberg. While there was some degree of tolerance for a pregnancy which was followed by a hasty marriage, there was little tolerance for situations where children were born to unmarried mothers, who found themselves in a very difficult position. Prior to the Industrial Revolution, many women worked at home and so it was possible to earn money and raise children at the same time.

By the middle of the twentieth century, however, workplace conditions in many Western countries dictated that women were forced to resign from their employment after their marriage, or else when they subsequently became pregnant. An unmarried expectant mother usually had to resign before her pregnancy became obvious. Had she chosen to raise her child, it would have been rare for her to be offered re-employment after the birth.

These conditions made it almost impossible for an unmarried mother to provide the necessary on-going financial support for herself and a child. In those days before access to education was available throughout people's lives, an unplanned pregnancy could also spell the end to the mother's educational opportunities. Lack of education would be likely to result in poorly paid employment, providing another reason why an unmarried mother would find it difficult to support herself and a child.

The belief in the Protestant work ethic led to the transfer of many children of unmarried mothers to married couples, who were expected to be able to support them financially and give them more opportunities in life. Many unmarried mothers felt guilty and apologetic, because they were bringing a child into the world for whom they could not provide financial support. They had failed to comply with the demands of the Protestant work ethic. The expectation that adults would provide for themselves also meant that many unmarried expectant mothers were required to pay their way, either in cash or by working for their accommodation, in homes for unmarried mothers, or in private accommodation, often caring for other people's children.

Attachment theory

The influential beliefs which contributed to the mass of the adoption iceberg were founded not only in religion, but also in psychology. The adoption iceberg was made much more robust by adding the element which represented belief in 'attachment theory'.

When the Second World War broke out, in 1939, Dr John Bowlby, a British psychologist, appealed to the British government not to allow children under the age of five years to be evacuated without their mothers. After the war, when many children in Britain were left without homes and parents, Dr Bowlby was asked by the World Health Organisation to develop a report on the needs of those children. By 1958 (coincidentally the date of the earliest account in *Adoption Separation*) he had formulated the foundation for what would become known as attachment theory.

Prior to 1958, it appears from the available information that there were fewer children born to unmarried mothers, but a higher percentage of those children were raised within their families of origin.

Bowlby's theory was presented in a three-volume series, published between 1969 and 1982 and its impact was substantial. His work was supported by psychologist Anna Freud (daughter of Sigmund), who found that the British children who had remained in the major cities with their families during the war, instead of being evacuated to the country to live with strangers, had fared better, not only emotionally, but also physically.

Put very simply, Bowlby proposed that infants require 'a continuous, warm relationship' with a mother or mother figure and that if this does not occur in the very early period of life, then there is a likelihood of long term mental health issues in adulthood. Bowlby's theories around attachment were accepted by governments in many countries and led to the gradual closure of orphanages and institutions and to more emphasis being placed on foster care and adoption for children unable to be raised by their parents.

Bowlby's views on the importance of early attachment led to a widespread belief that children would suffer long term adverse consequences, if they were not cared for on a fulltime basis in their early years, by one person; that person being their mother or a substitute mother figure. This created a genuine fear, which is apparent in the narratives contained in *Adoption Separation*, that any children denied this care would grow up to become delinquents and display anti-social behaviour. Because of the acceptance of Bowlby's views, very few infants, in the middle of the twentieth century, were cared for by strangers.

In the United Kingdom, in the 1960s, some children were cared for in day care centres. However, this type of care was considered to be so unfortunate and inappropriate for children, that the only children who qualified for places there were those who were at risk of being removed from their parents because of neglect or abuse. These centres existed only so that those disadvantaged children could be placed there by the authorities for their own protection. In the twenty-first century, in contrast, many young children of quite competent parents spend long hours being cared for by an array of strangers in child-care centres.

Unless unmarried expectant mothers had someone on whom they could rely for financial support after the birth, they were considered to be unable to provide their children with the full time nurturing in their early years, which would allow them to develop good, long-term emotional and mental health. They were therefore judged by many to be unfit to raise children, which is why many hospitals required them to see the almoner (the name by which a hospital social worker was known in the United Kingdom) as soon as possible, so that options could be explored. Many unmarried mothers were persuaded by the powerful beliefs about attachment theory with which they were presented and accepted that adoption was going to be the way to ensure that their children would not grow up to develop the mental health issues predicted by Dr Bowlby.

Pregnancy and birthing experiences

From the accounts contained in *Adoption Separation*, it is clear that, for many unmarried mothers, the realisation of the pregnancy came as a shock, as there was very little preparation or education for young people around sexual behaviour. In many cases, expectant mothers struggled alone through the months of pregnancy, trying to imagine what the outcome might be for themselves and their children.

If they were not able to use the time between the confirmation of the pregnancy and the birth of the child to put in place plans and arrangements, which would allow them to raise their children, they were very vulnerable to coercion. If they presented at a hospital or a home for unmarried mothers, alone and unsupported, then it often seemed clear to those responsible for their care that no appropriate plans had been made for mother and child to stay together.

By not providing evidence of such plans for the future, these mothers were often assumed, by default, to have planned for their babies to be adopted. There is evidence of this in both hospital and social work department files of the time. Some records indicate that mothers were 'compliant' with the adoption process; this may have been partly because they had been raised to respect and obey those in authority and partly because they could envisage no viable alternative.

Staff in hospitals and homes for unmarried mothers brought with them to their work their own belief systems and values. Those who had the responsibility to care for these mothers generally believed that adoption was the most beneficial outcome for their children. For some of those workers, that certainty gave them a particular comfort and security, which allowed them to distance themselves from the mothers and objectify them as delinquent and inferior.

In some cases, Christianity provided a degree of confidence and self-righteousness, which allowed workers to justify discrimination against unmarried mothers and their children in harsh and punitive ways. Some workers felt that the whole experience should be as uncomfortable for the mother as possible, in order to deter her from repeating what they considered to be immoral and irresponsible behaviour. Many mothers experienced this treatment by staff as humiliating and demeaning.

In residential homes, mothers were sometimes locked in and only allowed to leave under supervision. They were seldom allowed to make telephone calls or have visitors and sometimes their mail was censored. It was rare for unmarried mothers in any setting to receive any preparation for either the physical or emotional issues around childbirth, far less preparation for the forthcoming separation from their child and its long term impact. They were generally prevented from attending ante-natal classes, where these were available. In some cases, places in homes for unmarried mothers were only available to women who had already committed themselves to proceed with adoption.

There was a wide range of opinions on the most appropriate care of unmarried mothers and their babies in the immediate post-natal period. There were those who believed that keeping mother and baby together for some time after the birth would be best for both. Babies would get the best possible start in life, with their mothers and those mothers would be forced to face the reality of the outcome of their actions and not totally escape the consequences, which would ensure that they did not repeat their irresponsible behaviour. However, there were also those who believed that parting mother and baby as early as possible would make the adjustment to separation easier for both and allow the babies to form a healthy and unambiguous attachment with the women who were to become their surrogate mothers.

There was also a fear that if the mother was allowed to spend time with her baby after the birth, she may develop such an attachment to the child that she would rashly refuse to allow the adoption to proceed, thereby condemning the child to a life of poverty and disadvantage – and, according to Bowlby, possible long term mental health issues. Some workers genuinely believed that the less involved the mother was with the process of birthing and motherhood, the easier it would be for her to recover from her experience, put it behind her and 'get on with her life'. During this period of time following the birth, it was common for mothers and babies both to be isolated, lonely and uncomforted. The long term impact of this period in their lives has been significant in many cases.

There were also those who interpreted Dr Bowlby's work to mean that the best outcome was for children to be raised by their mothers. Some homes for unmarried mothers, therefore, had a policy that babies remain with their mothers for a set period, in order to allow the mothers to recover from the birth and be in a better position to consider the future for their children. Sometimes fathers and grandparents, who had refused to support the mother throughout the pregnancy, had a change of heart, when they were personally introduced to the child. As a result, some mother ships were rescued at the last minute and the mother and child found their way into a lifeboat.

The dominant issues for many mothers were the disempowerment and lack of self-determination which they experienced, at a time of extreme emotional vulnerability. Rarely were they allowed to choose whether or not to see their baby, to name their baby or to nurse their baby. Some were even forced to deliver while under a general anaesthetic. This practice was intended to prevent post-natal bonding of mother and child. In situations where the father of the child may have wished to be included, he was often prevented by family and professionals from any involvement.

There is no doubt that some of those in positions of power took opportunities to abuse it. In some cases, organisations abused their power, such as the horrific history of the Magdalene Laundries in Ireland, which operated from the late eighteenth century until 1996.

Many thousands of women were incarcerated for the flimsiest of reasons, often for many years, in Magdalene Laundries, which operated in the twentieth century as adoption agencies. We also know from the accounts of mothers, that in other cases individuals abused their power in a variety of ways.

Availability of financial assistance in Australia

During the Second World War, in 1942, a Widow's Pension was made available in Australia, but originally only to a genuine widow or to a 'deserted wife' under certain circumstances. It was rarely made available to unmarried mothers, partly because there was a fear in the community that if benefits were too readily available for unmarried mothers, that this would encourage irresponsibility and sexual immorality.

In some families, children, regardless of their legitimacy, were valued to the extent that a way would be found for them to remain in the family. In such cases, some government assistance was available. A Special Benefit could be paid, but this was a short term payment, not designed to take the place of a permanent income. Family Allowance was payable to unmarried mothers, but this was a small payment, intended to supplement, not to replace a steady income. These government allowances, however, could assist a family to support an unmarried mother and her child, if the family chose to do so.

Then, in the early 1970s, unmarried mothers in Australia, with the support of the Council for the Single Mother and her Child, began to lobby the federal government to provide financial support for them, in order that their children could experience the same emotional benefits as the children of married mothers and widows. In 1973, new legislation was introduced which meant that unmarried mothers were entitled to a Supporting Mothers Benefit.

Since that time, single mothers have been able to provide their young children with the necessary nurturing, while the government provides the necessary financial support. The name of the payment was changed in 1977 to Supporting Parents Benefit, when single fathers became eligible. The payment is now known as a Parenting Payment. Recipients are required to seek child support, where appropriate and so the responsibility of both parents to provide for children is acknowledged.

Percentage of illegitimate children who were adopted

Although not all unmarried mothers of this era lost their children to adoption, it is impossible to determine what percentage of them did actually raise their children as single mothers, because of the way in which personal details were recorded in countries such as Australia.

Mothers who were living in de facto, or common-law marriage situations were, nevertheless, legally unmarried and their children were recorded as illegitimate. Those children, who were actually raised in a family situation by both of their parents, would be counted among the ones who were not adopted.

Also some unmarried mothers who remained within the family were still not allowed to raise their children, because many illegitimate children were separated from their mothers and raised by another relative, whom they grew up to regard as their mother. Those children also would be counted among those who were not adopted.

This means that a comparison between the number of adoptions and the number of illegitimate children born in this period does not provide an accurate picture of the percentage of illegitimate children who were raised by single mothers.

However, we now have considerable evidence from the unmarried mothers whose children were adopted, which indicates that most of those mothers did not have financial support from either the fathers of their children or their own parents, which would have allowed them to be full-time carers to their infants.

The number of mother ships which came to grief on the adoption iceberg could have been reduced, if adequate financial support from the government had become available at an earlier date.

The dilemma

Unmarried mothers, as portrayed in *Adoption Separation*, were judged to be guilty of acting both immorally, by violating the prescribed sexual code of conduct and irresponsibly, by breaching the Protestant work ethic. They were therefore considered to have failed themselves and their children on both counts. They often found themselves shamed and blamed by families, friends, religious organisations and welfare professionals.

Even if they felt strong enough to withstand the community disapproval, which could have a long term impact on their own lives as well as the lives of their children, they still faced an insoluble dilemma.

In order to fulfil their responsibilities under the Protestant work ethic ideal, they would be forced to transgress the attachment theory ideal. If they planned to provide for their children financially, they were going to be unable to provide for them emotionally.

Because of this, the strong message, which they encountered both directly and indirectly from many sources, was that if they loved their children, they would agree for them to be adopted, rather than selfishly try to raise them and thereby condemn them to a life of both financial and emotional disadvantage. In this way, their love for their children was used as a weapon against their motherhood. Any unmarried father who considered raising his child would have been faced with the same dilemma.

Because of the apparently insoluble nature of this dilemma, many unmarried mothers felt that they were being forced by circumstances to consent to adoption, in spite of the fact that they had no way of knowing what the long term outcomes would be, for themselves or for their children. Many unmarried mothers were placed in a powerless situation and were therefore unable to assert themselves in defence of their motherhood. In most cases, the question which was presented to them was not whether they wanted to raise their children, but whether or not they wanted what was 'best for their children' - which was, of course, defined for them by others.

It was very difficult for individual mother ships to circumvent the adoption iceberg, because of its massive destructive power. The result was that many loving mothers were prevented from raising their children, in spite of the fact that they had not shown any indication of being incompetent. Many did, in fact, go on to become very competent parents to subsequent children. However, they often felt diminished by the experience which resulted in the loss of what was, for most, their first child and, for some, their only child.

For some mothers, the separation from their child became permanent. They were prevented from discovering the whereabouts of their child initially by the child's name being legally changed. The rationale for this may have been based on a fear that when the mother was able to recover from the birth and consider the reality of her relationship with her child, she may have been able to find a way out of her dilemma and then attempt to claim back her child. This policy of changing the child's legal identity and concealing that new identity suggests an unacknowledged awareness that many mothers did not part with their children voluntarily and that, if support had become available, they may have attempted to reclaim and raise their children.

In the majority of the geographical locations represented in *Adoption Separation*, mothers are still prevented, when their children become adults, from accessing the legal documents which would give them this information and allow them to attempt to trace their adult children. It seems to some mothers that they are doomed to be permanently punished for having been forced by circumstances into 'doing the right thing'.

There is a painful irony in the fact that they were considered to be responsible enough when they were much younger to make a life-altering decision, but it seems that once their children are adults, those same mothers cannot be trusted to have information about their children's identities.

Conclusion

Societal changes in the countries represented in *Adoption Separation* have to a large extent resolved the dilemma which was faced by unmarried mothers in earlier times. Religious beliefs have been robustly challenged and the power of religion to define people's convictions has diminished. This has led to a more liberal attitude towards sexual behaviour. The efforts of the Feminist movement have helped to improve equity for women in the workforce. Because many parents whose lives have been affected by adoption separation have been brave and generous enough to share their experiences, we have learned from the errors and horrors of the past. Society has also benefited from learning of the experiences of those who were adopted and of the long term impact on them of being separated from their families of origin.

It is rare nowadays for mothers in the countries represented in the book to be discriminated against with regard to ante-natal and post-natal care on the basis of their marital status. The result for all of those countries, Australia in particular, has been that very few mothers and children are separated by adoption in the twenty-first century, for the reasons which prevailed in the past.

Many thousands of parents and children in those countries, however, are still suffering because they were separated by adoption. As a result, several state and territory governments in Australia have issued formal apologies to all those whose lives have been adversely affected by the past adoption policies and practices described in *Adoption Separation*. In 2013 we expect an apology from the Australian Federal Government. These apologies attest to the fact that the policies and practices which resulted in so many family separations were both harmful and indefensible.

However, there are still countries around the world in which many mother ships are foundering on adoption icebergs.

Adoption and Loss

Since the middle of the twentieth century, hundreds of thousands of children have been removed from their mothers and families in countries such as the Philippines and the Republic of Korea to be adopted into other countries, including Australia. Unmarried mothers around the world are still feeling that they are being forced by circumstances to part with their children. Their experiences are very similar to those for which Australians are currently receiving apologies.

Australia has acknowledged the damage caused by unnecessary separations of children from their families. We also have a responsibility to assist those countries, in which this is still occurring, to develop solutions, which will meet the needs of families who find themselves in difficulties. We must cease to support the unjustifiable removal of children from their mothers, anywhere in the world.

Australia must now bow to increasing national and international pressure to consider further apologies for having continued to support the insupportable in other countries.

~~~~~~

Part Two

The grief caused by adoption loss

Adoption and Loss

Chapter 1 Grief experienced by original mothers

Grief is the emotional reaction to a loss. There are losses other than death which give rise to grief reactions. It is now obvious that a serious loss is experienced by the mothers who give birth to children who are then adopted by someone else. The grief of the original mother of a child who has been adopted is a unique experience and differs in fundamental ways from other grief experiences. Although the fathers of children lost through adoption often grieve also, as do the grandparents, siblings and other members of the extended families, their grief has its own qualities and is not the same as that of the mother who has physically carried her child and given birth, but has been unable to follow through and raise her child.

One of the reasons that the relationship between original mothers and their adopted children has gone unrecognised is that the depth of the connection between the expectant mother and her unborn child has been underestimated. There was a view that it was advisable that children who were to be adopted should be removed from their mothers before a relationship between mother and child was able to develop. This attitude failed to recognise the fact that such a relationship had already developed prior to the birth of the child. Many women whose children were subsequently adopted were prevented from seeing them and were sometimes lied to and told that their child had died. These actions were illegal, of course, as prior to the adoption order being granted, the original mother was still the child's legal parent and had every right to act as such without hindrance. Original mothers were often unaware of their legal rights, however after having been systematically disempowered throughout their pregnancies.

Until recent years, similar steps were taken in cases of stillbirth and neo-natal death. Babies were often removed before the mothers were able to see them, many mothers were not allowed to name their children and generally no funeral was arranged. Nowadays, women who have lost children to stillbirth or neo-natal death are encouraged to hold their children, to have photographs taken, to keep mementoes such as locks of hair and handprints, to name their children and to talk about them.

Original mothers of adopted children have traditionally lacked a concrete focus for their grief as many of those whose children are now adults were not allowed to see their babies prior to being separated from them and many were prevented from caring for their children prior to the adoption being finalised. Many original mothers were not even allowed to name their babies and they were not given a birth certificate as evidence that they had actually had a child.

In cases of stillbirth and neo-natal death, bonding is now actively encouraged, as it is believed that this actually facilitates the grieving process. In most cases of adoption, in the past, systematic attempts were made after birth to prevent bonding, although this had already occurred regardless of these efforts. In more recent times, women whose children were to be adopted have been encouraged to spend time with them before the separation, but it is not known as yet whether or not this has had a significant impact on the long term grief that they suffer.

In the middle of the twentieth century, when so many newborn children were taken from their mothers to be adopted, there was no historical body of evidence in relation to the long term outcomes for either those mothers, or their children. The reasons for the lack of research are that prior to the 1960s, stranger adoptions were rare and secrecy was common. This meant that there was no motivation for academics to study the long term outcomes of adoption separation. Many adoptions of infants took place in the United Kingdom, Ireland, Australia, New Zealand, the United States and Canada in the second half of the twentieth century in the absence of any body of knowledge about the likely long term outcomes for all concerned.

In 1979, Joss Shawyer, wrote a book called *Death by Adoption*. In 1969, Shawyer was unmarried and pregnant with twins. She was appalled at the assumption that she would agree for her twins to be adopted and horrified at the pressure that was placed on her when she refused. Shawyer's book was ground-breaking as it viewed adoption as a women's issue and explored the values underpinning adoption. Shawyer described adoption as, '...a violent act, a political act of aggression towards a woman who has supposedly offended the sexual mores by committing the unforgivable act of not suppressing her sexuality'.

According to Shawyer the punishment for this unforgivable act is, 'She is stripped of her child by a variety of subtle and not so subtle manoeuvres and then brutally abandoned'. Shawyer describes social workers who arranged the adoptions as, 'Specially trained state-employed personnel...(who)...police her fall from grace and arrange to remove the product of her transgression to a safe and secret place'. Shawyer describes how immature, unmarried mothers were persuaded to allow their children to be given to infertile, married women, supposedly 'for their own good'. Shawyer tells the stories not just of original mothers, but also of adopted people. Her book also includes an interview with an adoptive mother and an interview with an involuntarily childless woman who did not adopt. Their stories are riveting, although often tragic.

In 1981, Phyllis Silverman wrote a book *entitled Helping Women Cope with Grief* (1981). This is one of a few books that directly tackles the issue of the grief of original mothers directly.

147

Adoption and Loss

In the introduction to her book, she points out that she is addressing the issues of women who have found themselves in situations, '...for which their previous experience has not prepared them'. Her book is directed at those in the helping professions. Silverman describes how so many original mothers suppressed their grief and how this suppressed grief manifested itself in feelings of guilt, anger, tenseness and fear of discovery. Silverman goes on to say that, '...the pain, secrecy and guilt involved in their experience can profoundly affect their future marriages'. Silverman also points out that some original mothers later marry in order to gain approval from parents, who, '...had expressed disappointment or disgust with their previous pregnancies'.

Silverman describes the impact of breaking the secrecy as a 'thawing out' as original mothers sometimes describe themselves after disclosing their status, '...as having been in a deep freeze, sometimes for years'. Silverman acknowledges the crucial importance of support groups for original mothers and says that, 'Without such an understanding and sympathetic forum, many birthmothers would remain in hiding, postponing or even indefinitely deferring their accommodation to their grief'.

Among those who have addressed the grief and loss issues of mothers who have lost children through adoption are Robin Winkler and Margaret van Keppel. Winkler and van Keppel presented a paper at the Third Australian Adoption Conference in 1982. In this paper they compared the loss of a child through adoption with other losses and pointed out its two main distinguishing features.

The first is the fact that the original mother often feels responsible for the fact that her child was adopted and therefore feels the loss as a self-inflicted one. This results in feelings of guilt, shame and powerlessness. The second is that the child is lost to the mother, but still lives and so there is always the possibility of a reunion. This means that there is a lack of finality to the loss. According to Winkler and van Keppel, these are the two most important factors, which make resolution of the original mother's grief exceptionally difficult.

In 1984, Winkler and van Keppel conducted a study of two hundred and thirteen women, Australia-wide, who had lost a first child through adoption. They found that the effects of the loss of the child on the mother were both negative and long lasting. All of the women who participated in the study reported a sense of loss, which did not diminish over time. In fact, approximately half of the women surveyed reported an increase in the sense of loss over time. The women involved in the Winkler and van Keppel study were, of course, all volunteers, most of whom responded to requests in the media.

Original mothers such as these, who are prepared to discuss their experiences and feelings, have obviously already made some adjustment to their situation compared to those who have not yet addressed their loss issues and are still operating under the burden of silence and suppression. Winkler and van Keppel's results, therefore, could represent an under-estimation of the negative effects of the loss of a child through adoption on mothers.

In 1984 also, Kate Inglis wrote a book called *Living Mistakes*, which is sub-titled, *Women who consented to adoption*. Her book grew out of her observation that women who were recounting their reproductive histories and revealed that they had lost a child through adoption, '...exhibited a pattern of behaviour in the telling which centred on an unresolved grief and an ambivalence about their motherhood'.

Inglis goes on to say that, 'Their isolation in both the event and the memory was striking'. Inglis states that while anger is a common response to loss and a recognised component of grief, 'Anger is also a likely consequence following relinquishment'. She goes on to describe many of the ways in which original mothers are angry and many of the ways in which that anger can be expressed. She also acknowledges that in many

149

cases it remains unexpressed. Inglis says of the original mother, 'She may begin her pregnancy in anger and resentment and continue for years with a randomly placed rage'.

Dr John Condon of Flinders Medical Centre, South Australia, conducted some research in 1986. The results of his South Australian study of twenty natural mothers support Winkler and van Keppel's conclusions. Condon found, '...a very high incidence of pathological grief reactions which have failed to resolve although many years have elapsed since the relinquishment'. Condon also recorded that more than half of the women he surveyed reported that their anger had increased since the time of relinquishment. This was further evidence that time alone was not resolving the grief of original mothers.

In a paper called *The Experience of Loss in Adoption*, presented at the Fifth National Conference, National Association for Loss and Grief, in Perth, Western Australia, in September, 1987, van Keppel, Midford and Cicchini presented a paper in which they pointed out that there were often additional stressful life-events connected with the loss of a child through adoption). Many original mothers had to move to another residence or sometimes to another town during their pregnancy in order to avoid the shame and embarrassment for themselves and their families. For many, the pregnancy meant the end of their relationship with the father of their child. Some were forced by the pregnancy to leave study or employment.

The pregnancy caused an irreversible change in the relationship between the original mother and her parents, whether the parents were aware of the pregnancy or not. The pregnancy often drove a wedge between the expectant mother and her friends. Original mothers often resented their friends for their freedom and their hopes for the future. As a result of these changes, many original mothers felt very isolated at the time of their pregnancies. Most original mothers were immature and unable to cope with this combination of stressful events all occurring at the same time. After enduring the pregnancy, often in social isolation, many were then required to make a decision regarding their child's future. Van Keppel, Midford and Cicchini also noted that, 'It is not uncommon for birth mothers to experience difficulties in forming or maintaining significant relationships' and they relate this to the fact that the relinquishment of the child was coupled with other emotional events.

All of this research contributed to a growing awareness of the long term grief and loss issues for mothers who had been separated from their children by adoption. around Australia, those mothers began to form support groups and have worked individually and collectively for many years to educate and inform the general public and politicians.

For my part, I presented conference papers and information and training sessions in Australia and in other countries between 1995 and 2010.

Chapter 2 Grief experienced by adopted people

Throughout the twentieth century, very little attention was paid to the grief experienced by adopted people. Some references have been made to adoptions which had unhappy outcomes for the adopted children, for example where the adoption was terminated by the adoptive parents and the child returned to care, or where the child was abused by the adoptive parents. These unhappy situations are more common than many people would like to admit. There are even situations where unwanted adopted children are 'advertised' on the internet to be 'rehomed' ie re-adopted. In many cases, however, the painful consequences of adoption are less obvious.

Only in recent years has come the realisation that adopted people, regardless of how apparently problem-free their adoptions have been, can experience a deep and painful sense of loss because they have been separated from their original parents and families. Their grief resulting from this loss is not always obvious because it has usually been suppressed and is often exhibited indirectly in the behaviour of adopted people, especially in the adolescent years.

If the grief is not addressed appropriately, however, the behaviours can continue on into adulthood. Adopted people, like their original mothers, have not been encouraged by society to express their grief as the expectation was that they would be grateful to their adoptive parents for 'rescuing' them. Society has traditionally admired adoptive parents for doing what appeared to be a community service by adopting children who were thought to be without families. In fact, these children did have families and they have spent their lives separated from them. We are now aware that many adoptions which took place in the twentieth century were not conducted ethically and some were, in fact, illegal.

For many adopted people, the fact that they were not raised by their natural mothers causes them to feel rejected and abandoned. They suffer from the loss of their relationship with their original mothers, the loss of kinship by being separated from their extended families and community and the loss of identity from not knowing exactly who they are. These losses are particularly obvious in the cases of cross-cultural adoptions.

This was very poignantly illustrated by Dr Joyce Maguire Pavao at the Adoption and Healing Conference in New Zealand in 1997. Dr Pavao is an adopted person and a family therapist. She told the story of a young man called Trevor who attempted suicide when he was thirteen years old. Trevor had been adopted from Colombia when he was four years old by an American family, described by Pavao as, '...very affluent, a white family who lived in a beautiful suburb of Boston'. Dr Pavao tried to help the young man find a reason to go on living. His response to her was, 'You don't understand, Joyce, I can't live. I'm dead. I have been dead since I was four or five years old. My name was Ricardo. I spoke Spanish. I lived in another country, I was another person and I have been trying very hard to be this new person and I can't do it, I just can't do it'.

Our society has found it difficult to accept that adoption may have caused more problems than it has ever solved and there is still a great deal of resistance in the community to acknowledging the damage caused by adoption. Fortunately, more and more research is being done, however, on the outcomes for adopted people, although even those who have exposed the unhappy results of adoption have difficulty understanding that the pain caused to adopted people is not inevitable and that society does not simply have to tolerate it.

Adopted people, like their original mothers, lack a concrete focus for their grief, as they usually have no conscious memory of those mothers. There is also no finality to their grief, as they know that they have other families somewhere and that they will always, in some way, be a part of those families. Adopted people lack any rituals to facilitate their grieving, as they were usually not intellectually aware at the time that the adoption took place. Even if they are told that they are adopted, many questions and mysteries remain. Like their original mothers, they have often not expressed their true feelings of loss and so too often the assumption has been that those feelings did not exist.

As their original mothers appeared to 'get on with their lives' and often showed no outward signs of their inner turmoil, so adopted people often appear to be content with their lot and show no obvious signs of grieving. This does not mean, of course, that they do not suffer.

An article called *The Painful Legacy of Adoption* appeared in *The Age* newspaper in Melbourne, Australia, in June 1993. It was written by journalist Louise Bellamy. Ms Bellamy reported that she had interviewed Brother Alex McDonald who had worked with homeless young people in St Kilda in Melbourne for ten years. Ms Bellamy reported Brother McDonald as saying that, '...of the 147 suicides of young people caused by drugs and abuse in the area over the past decade, 142 came from adoption backgrounds'.

Nancy Verrier is an adoptive mother and a clinical psychologist. She presented a paper at the American Adoption Congress International Convention in 1991 and, in 1993, expanded it into a book called *The Primal Wound*. Verrier spoke at the convention of the 'staggering' statistics which show that although adopted people make up 2-3% of the population in the

The Hidden Grief

United States, they make up 30-40% of the young people in 'special schools, juvenile hall and residential treatment centres'. In this paper, Verrier described how the adopted person's perception of having been abandoned by their original mother often affects their feelings of self-worth in a negative way and causes them to have a constant fear of further abandonment. Verrier explained that this fear of abandonment results in hyper-vigilance on the part of the child, which is why so many adopted people suffer from free-floating anxiety and psychosomatic illnesses, especially unexplained stomach-aches, headaches and allergies.

Verrier spoke of the separation of the child from the original mother as an experience 'from which neither fully recovers' and said that the adopted person, in losing the sense of well-being and security of the presence of their original mother, had 'lost something which could never be regained'. Verrier also spoke about the phenomenon of adopted people sabotaging their birthdays, because the anniversary for them represents sorrow and parting, not joy. In this paper, Verrier also explained that adopted people often apparently make a 'good adjustment' to their adoption, but what this means is simply that they learn how to seek approval and to suppress their true feelings.

Verrier wrote in 1993 of the pain experienced by adopted people and of the difficulties of finding professionals who are aware of the issues for adoptive families. In *The Primal Wound* she describes how many adoptive parents believe that all their adopted children need is to be loved and how, as adopted children grow up, parents often have difficulty understanding their testing-out behaviour. One of the reasons that there has been little recognition of the needs of adopted people is the lack of understanding of the bond between mother and child which grows during pregnancy and the resultant impact on the child of the separation from the mother.

Some adoptive parents who have never had natural children of their own find it difficult to understand the importance

155

of this bond. Verrier, however, has had her own natural child and so perhaps this has made it easier for her to appreciate the bond that develops during pregnancy. Verrier also explains that she finally came to understand that it is sometimes difficult for adopted children to accept the love that their adoptive parents want to give them and that this testing-out behaviour is, '…one of two diametrically opposed responses to being abandoned, the other being a tendency toward acquiescence, compliance and withdrawal'. Verrier says that it sometimes takes years of therapy for adopted people to get in touch with their feelings of rejection.

Verrier found that adopted people were, 'greatly over-represented in psychotherapy', that they '…demonstrated a high incidence of juvenile delinquency, sexual promiscuity and running away from home' and that they consistently showed symptoms which were 'impulsive, provocative, aggressive and antisocial'.

Verrier writes about the difference between attachment and bonding. She says that adopted children form an attachment to their adoptive parents because they quickly come to realise that their survival depends on it, but that they may never truly bond with them.

Verrier points out that bonding begins in the womb and is exhibited by the fact that, in the crucial period immediately following birth, new-born babies have been shown to recognise their mothers, through smell, heartbeat, voice and eye contact. The child is born with the expectation that its life will revolve around the person with whom it has become familiar for nine months.

When this does not happen, when this continuum is broken by the child suddenly being handled by a different person ie the adoptive mother, the baby can be left feeling, '...hopeless, helpless, empty, and alone'. Verrier goes on to state that, '...the severing of that connection.....causes a primal or narcissistic wound.....which manifests in a sense of loss, basic mistrust, anxiety and depression, emotional and/or behavioural problems, and difficulties in relationships with significant others'.

156

The Hidden Grief

Betty Jean Lifton is an adopted person and the author of several books on adoption topics. In 1994, Lifton wrote *Journey of the Adopted Self*, in which she explores the impact of adoption on adopted people. Lifton also describes the two opposing responses of adopted people, which are particularly noticeable during adolescence, when she describes the compliant adopted people who, because of their issues of unresolved grief and loss, '...pay the price with eating disorders, phobias, and an underlying depression' while others, '...take an oppositional stance to anyone who tries to control them, be they parents, school teachers, or legal authorities'. In many families where there are two adopted children, it is common for one child to be compliant and the other to be rebellious. This was described to me by one adoptive mother as, *One shuts up, the other acts up*.

Lifton goes on to say that adopted children, '...often do not feel entitled to express any negative feelings, such as grief or anger at being cut off from their origins' and points out that this anger often displays as depression. It also, however, often, 'manifests itself in destructive, acting-out behaviour'. Lifton gives as a possible cause of the over-representation of adopted people in psychiatric wards, '...the difficulty many young adoptees have repressing their grief and anger and sense of powerlessness' and says, 'Therapists should not be asking why adopted children are angry, but why shouldn't they be?'. Lifton also points out that many adoptive parents find these ideas threatening. She says, 'The need to idealize the institution of adoption in order to ward off their own fears unfortunately prevents these parents from being in touch with their children's pain'.

Lifton also writes about the outcomes associated with adoption and the, '...high psychic cost that both parent and child pay when they repress their grief and loss'. She goes on to say that, in her opinion, '...it is unnatural for members of the human species to grow up separated from...their natural clan' and that because of the effects of this separation on adopted people, 'They grow up feeling like anonymous people cut off from the genetic and social heritage that gives everyone else roots'. Lifton is aware that this news is not often well received by adoptive parents. She cautions them that if they love their children they will have empathy for the sorrow that they experience not, '...turn on the professionals who describe it'. Lifton writes about adopted people being 'strong enough' to claim their heritage, when they search for their original parents and describes how in children who have been adopted, lack of knowledge about their origins 'interferes with the child's struggle to form an early sense of self' and that '...not even the most loving adoptive parents...can soften the psychic toll that...exacts from the child'.

Lifton describes how an Artificial Self is created. She describes the Artificial Self as being '...compliant, afraid to express its real feelings, such as sadness or anger, for fear of losing the only family it has'. In fact, Lifton suggests that the suffering of adopted children may begin before they are even born. Research now suggests that unborn children respond to sound and may be affected by the experiences and emotions of their mothers during pregnancy.

Lifton describes separation anxiety and how it exists in adoptive families. Many adopted people have difficulty separating from their adoptive parents, even to attend school. The reason these difficulties arise is that any separation resurrects the feelings of loss related to the earlier separation from the original mother. Lifton also says that some adopted people deliberately choose to become indispensable to their adoptive parents to ensure that they will not be abandoned by them and therefore not have to undergo yet another separation.

Children were often adopted to fulfil the desires and fantasies of their adoptive parents. Many adopted people, even into adulthood, feel an unhealthy responsibility for ensuring that their adoptive parents are happy. Some never outgrow the compliant attitude they practised as they were growing up. For other adoptees, the search for an identity leads them to choose a negative identity in order to associate with the impression they have obtained from their adoptive parents that their original parents were somehow defective.

Both Lifton and Verrier mention the fact that sexual promiscuity is common among adopted people. Lifton says, 'Both male and female adoptees give themselves freely to others out of a sense of worthlessness or as a way of trying to get close to another person. Physical intimacy gives them the illusion of love'. Lifton also mentions David Kirschner, who, she says, found that adopted people often exhibited, '...deceptive charm that covered over a shallowness of attachment'.

Joanne Small is an adopted person and a clinical social worker. She is the author of an article entitled, *Working with Adoptive Families*, which was published in a journal called *Public Welfare* in 1987. The article is sub-titled, *We must come to see that families who adopt are not the same as others*. Small describes how adoptive families operate to deny the difference between raising adopted children and raising one's own natural children. A result of this denial, according to Small, is that, '...the child's basic sense of self develops around a faulty belief system'. This is obviously damaging to the developing child who is trying to establish his or her identity and place in the family and in the world.

Small describes some of the characteristics of adoptive families, for example, family members have difficulty identifying and expressing their feelings about adoption, there is a tendency toward perfectionism and unrealistic expectations, fantasy replaces reality, there are feelings of powerlessness, members of the family feel responsible for the feelings of others, members of the family share low self esteem and family members show a strong need for approval.

Small writes about the confusion created in the minds of adopted children who are told by their adoptive parents that their original mothers gave them away because they loved them. Children know that people do not give away that which they value. When their adoptive mothers then tell them that they love them also, there is an underlying fear that they too may one day give them away. Who would say, for example, *I love my husband/wife so much that I'm going to give him/her to you*? It makes no sense. How then, do we expect children to accept that it was because their mothers loved them so much that they gave them away to other mothers to raise?

Small also describes the denial which exists among professionals who work with adopted people of the importance in their lives of having been adopted. Small says, 'We must recognize the role of denial among professionals working with adoptive families, some of whom are themselves members of adoptive families and many of whom are unwittingly engaged in codependent roles'. Small calls for training to be provided to professionals, which should include, '...an understanding of the differences in adoptive family structure, the role of denial in adoptive families, the meaning and effects of codependence on professionals and adoptive family members' among other factors.

Small describes the denial practised by adopted people. She says, 'Adult children of adoption also carry with them a strong tendency to deny that adoption can be the basis for their problems'. Small goes on to describe how adopted people can let go of this denial by searching for their original parents. Small says that, 'Adult children who search have chosen to give up the denial'. Small recommends that adopted people attend support groups in order to share their experiences and gain strength from the support of others who have also been adopted. In this way their innermost feelings can be validated and not denied.

In some countries a stepparent is allowed to adopt the child of his or her partner. In most cases the original parent, with whom the child no longer lives, signs an adoption consent. In all cases, as with all adoptions, the child's name is changed and the original birth certificate declared null and void. Many children who have been adopted by stepparents have the same sorts of issues that other adopted children have. They have a parent who has lost the right to parent them and they have grown up with at least one parent to whom they are not genetically related. Children adopted by stepparents have also been issued with a new, false birth certificate and have lost their original identities.

Their original parent, whom they may have known and loved, is, after the adoption, no longer legally related to them. Some of them have issues of abandonment and low self-esteem. Some have issues of identity and belonging.

There is no justification for stepparent adoptions. Matters of inheritance can be resolved by the making of a will and an adoption does not necessarily guarantee that a child will feel welcome in the newly created family. The passing of the *Adoption Act 1988* in South Australia virtually put an end to stepparent adoptions.

While there is no avoiding the fact that adopted people are more likely to find themselves in psychiatric care, there is no way of knowing for sure why this is so. Some adoptive parents blame it on heredity, although anecdotal evidence suggests that subsequent children raised by original mothers do not require psychiatric help to the same degree. Some put it down to the fact that adoptive parents are more inclined to introduce their adopted children to psychiatric interaction.

While these factors may go some way towards explaining the over-representation of adopted people in psychiatric care, they do not necessarily explain the over-representation of adopted people in the prison system, among youth suicides and among the homeless. Considering what we know about attachment and identity, it is far more likely that the behaviours of adopted people are a reaction to the losses that they have experienced.

Research undertaken among adopted people shows that they grieve for the loss of their mothers and their original families and that this grief can affect their feelings of self-worth and their ability to form close relationships with other people.

Only when there is an end to the denial surrounding the damage caused by adoption will adopted people be able to receive appropriate help which acknowledges their grief and loss and supports them to work towards resolution.

Chapter 3 Grief counselling

Having established that original mothers and adopted people do grieve after their separation, it might be expected that they could be assisted by grief counselling. Much has been written about grief, its purpose and its expected course. For most people grief following a loss, such as a death, is productive ie it leads to resolution. In many cases grief counselling can be helpful in assisting people to come to terms with their loss. Suggestions for grief counselling are provided by J. William Worden in his book *Grief Counselling and Grief Therapy*, published in 1982.

Other writers on the topic offer similar advice for assisting those who are grieving. Worden believes that mourning is necessary after a loss in order to re-establish equilibrium and describes the four tasks which he believes should be completed in order to achieve the emotional healing which should follow mourning.

The first task described by Worden is acceptance of the reality of the loss. This is a difficult task for original mothers, as they often do not have any concrete focus for their grief. Many of them did not see their babies and after being separated from them they were given no formal acknowledgement of the child's birth or adoption. The denial practised by society in general of their experience and their existence also lends an air of unreality to the event. When their child is issued with a new, false birth certificate, which denies the existence of the original parents, this denial becomes official. Those who grieve a death must accept the irreversibility of the loss, but original mothers often dream that their child will return to them. This makes it difficult for them to accept the reality of the loss, because they can never know whether or not the separation is going to be permanent.

Accepting the reality of the loss is difficult for adopted people as they also lack a concrete focus for their grief. In most cases, they have no conscious memory of what they have lost in terms of their mother. What they have lost in terms of a possible life can only be guessed at, not measured. They have lost the possibility of being raised in their family of origin, but who is to know what that might have been like?

The very fact that adoption agencies in the past often tried to 'match' adopted children with the physical characteristics of the adoptive parents suggests that the intention was to facilitate a denial of the truth. Presented with a new birth certificate and a new identity, adopted people are unable to conceptualise the lost person, the person they could have been. Like their mothers, adopted people are aware that the lost families exist somewhere and so their loss, like that of their original mothers, is not final.

Worden's second task is that of experiencing the pain of grief. Worden states that if this pain is avoided or suppressed then the course of mourning will be prolonged. Worden also says that avoidance of conscious grieving often leads to depression. Because original mothers are often viewed by others as having voluntarily given up their children, their grief is not socially recognised and supported. They are not given permission to mourn at the time of their loss and so their grieving is usually postponed. Many original mothers are surprised at the depth of their pain many years after the event, when they are finally allowed to express their grief.

Adopted people are often expected to be grateful for being adopted and 'rescued' from their unhappy situation. When they speak up about their losses, which more and more of them have done, they are sometimes unjustly labelled 'ungrateful' or 'disloyal'. Many babies do, indeed, exhibit grief reactions at the time of their adoption, but there is also a need for adopted adults to be supported to understand their loss and to experience their grief.

Worden's third and fourth tasks are closely connected. The third task is that of adjusting to the environment from which the lost person is missing and the fourth task is to withdraw emotional energy and reinvest it in another relationship.

For original mothers the place of their lost child in their environment is one of expectation. The expectant mother is physically and emotionally prepared to take up the role of motherhood and to the mother whose child is adopted by someone else this role is denied.

Original mothers try to adjust to this fact in different ways. Many of them have another child, or other children, to try to fill the gap created by the lost child. Many original mothers, however, do not have any further children. They sometimes fear that another emotional attachment may also result in loss. Some feel that having been unable to raise one child, it would be disrespectful and disloyal to that first child to raise another child.

Some respond to their loss by distancing themselves from babies and young children, others take every opportunity to spend time with other people's babies. Original mothers live with the contradiction that they are mothers, but not mothers. They know that they have had a child, but they are expected to go on with their lives as if that child had not been born.

Adopted people vary in the ways in which they adjust to their new environment after adoption. Some try very hard to please, in order to feel safe in their relationship with their adoptive parents. Others are so afraid of further abandonment that they do not allow themselves to become close to anyone, thus protecting themselves from further hurt.

Adoption and Loss

Original mothers and adopted people are unable to perform the sorts of tasks that are expected following a loss, in order for grief resolution to proceed. It is obvious, therefore, that the standard formulae for grief counselling are not going to be appropriate for them. This does not mean, however, that they cannot be helped.

Some original mothers do consult professionals and request assistance in resolving their grief. Van Keppel, Midford and Cicchini stated at the Fifth National Conference, National Association for Loss and Grief, in Perth, Western Australia, in September, 1987, that they believed that there were ways for professionals to promote the adjustment of women who have lost children through adoption.

They suggest that grief counselling can be useful to original mothers and that this needs to be provided in an atmosphere of compassion and acceptance. They stress the importance of original mothers being given permission to express their feelings. Many adopted people also find it challenging to acknowledge feelings of loss and grief.

Writing in *Disenfranchised Grief*, edited by Kenneth Doka in 1989, David Meagher points out that, 'Grief that is absent, masked, or suppressed is abnormal and becomes pathological'. It is important for those in the helping professions to be aware, when working with original mothers and adopted people, that in many cases their grief has been suppressed for a long time and may, in fact, have become pathological. It is unreasonable, therefore, to expect short-term resolution.

Grief counselling can be very useful in helping original mothers to sort out where the responsibility lies. They can be assisted to explore to what extent they were responsible for the loss of their children and to what extent others were responsible.

With a better understanding of the pressures and motives involved, they can take responsibility for their own behaviours and realise that they are not responsible for the behaviours of others. Anger is a common component of grief. Original mothers need to be assured that their anger is justified and encouraged to express it in appropriate and productive ways. Productive expression of anger often leads to valuable changes being made.

There are also implications for the care of original mothers and adopted people who experience other losses in their lives. Because their adoption loss may remain unresolved, they often have great difficulty dealing with subsequent losses. Bereavement counsellors report that often those who are displaying lack of adaptation to a loss have, in fact, experienced a previous loss which remains unresolved, often because their grief in that previous situation was disenfranchised for some reason.

Those who counsel the bereaved report that they often find that women who are having difficulty coming to terms with a death will eventually admit to having previously experienced the loss of a child through adoption. The lack of resolution of this previous loss impedes their ability to come to terms with their current loss. This is not surprising, as, in many cases, the loss of the child through adoption was the first major loss in the life of the mother.

For adopted people, the loss of their relationship with their original mother happened at a time when they were unable to comprehend it, but not necessarily unable to experience it. For this reason it becomes for many of them also, an unresolved loss.

Fortunately there are now opportunities for those in the helping professions to be educated about the loss and grief associated with adoption separation. The Australian Psychological Society, for example, offers a training module on this topic, which includes many of the concepts which I initially introduced in this book in 2000.

For most of the twentieth century, before there was a broad acceptance of the loss and grief associated with adoption separation, original mothers were generally given either no help or inappropriate advice from professionals ie doctors, psychologists and social workers.

Adoption and Loss

Since their families and friends often were unable to help them, in many cases they struggled with their grief alone for many years. Adopted people also have in the past had great difficulty finding professional people who understood their issues.

In *Helping Women Cope with Grief*, Silverman describes the stages of grief as impact, recoil and accommodation. She describes how the role of the professional is to assist women to, '... remember the past and acknowledge and accept its influence on their futures'. She also recommends supplementing professional care with the mutual help experience. Silverman points to the incidence of depression in women and gives her opinion that the most common cause of this depression is the losses in women's lives and the way women deal with the grief which accompanies these losses.

Because original mothers were judged as having violated social taboos they became stigmatised and so incurred society's discomfort and disapproval. This corresponds with what many original mothers describe as the feeling that they don't 'fit' in society any more after losing their children through adoption. Because of this discomfort they may turn their feelings inward on themselves.

The result of this is often depression, because the grief remains unresolved. Many adopted people also have this feeling of 'not fitting' of always being 'different' and 'not belonging'. For them, this can also lead to depression and other psychological problems.

Silverman says about the original mother that, 'Instead of blaming society for denying her the right to mourn openly, she begins to blame herself for not being able to behave the way those around her would prefer'. Thus the original mother repeats her perceived failure. She has been judged to have failed society by breaking the taboo of sex outside of marriage and has then shattered the myth of supposed maternal dedication by 'giving away' her baby; she then compounds her sense of failure by not being able to return to her normal life as if nothing had happened, which is what she feels is expected of her.

Timing can be an important factor in post-adoption grief counselling. There are certain life events which may result in family members who have been separated by adoption seeking specific support around their adoption separation issues. Births and deaths often have a deep impact on those who have experienced adoption separation and can trigger a surge of adoption-related grief. For mothers, the births of subsequent children and grandchildren can be quite challenging.

For those who are adopted, the births of their own children can cause them to think more about their own birth. For mothers, the death of their parents may be particularly significant, especially if their parents played a major role in the loss of the child through adoption. For those who are adopted, the deaths of their adoptive parents can cause them to confront the fact that their original parents are mortal also and may still be alive, as traditionally adoptive parents tended to be significantly older than the original parents of the children they adopted. Although original mothers and adopted people do grieve and may benefit from grief counselling, their loss situation is complicated by the particular circumstances operating in adoption. Post Adoption Counselling is a specialised area and appropriate training and education should be provided for those employed in this field.

Following the National Apology for Forced Adoptions delivered in Australia in 2013, the Australian Government invested $11.5 million over four years to assist those affected by forced adoption practices, as part of its response to the recommendations in the *Senate Committee report on the Commonwealth Contribution to Former Forced Adoption Policies and Practices*. Since then, these funds have been used to provide post-adoption counselling around Australia, in most cases at no cost to clients. The organisations providing these services are independent and not linked to any government departments.

Chapter 4 The silence factor and the role of ritual

One of the simplest, yet most therapeutic ways of dealing with a loss is to talk about it to an empathetic listener. Unfortunately, most people did not want to hear about the feelings of mothers who had lost children through adoption and these mothers did not expect people to be empathetic. Many original mothers of adopted children kept their loss a secret, because of the possible social repercussions and suffered in silence. In many cases, the result of this was that their loss was never discussed at all. This generally prevented or postponed the resolution of their grief.

Kenneth Doka is the editor of a book entitled, *Disenfranchised Grief*, which is subtitled, *Recognizing Hidden Sorrow* (1989). This book is very useful for those trying to understand grief caused by adoption separation.

In *Disenfranchised Grief*, Dale Kuhn discusses the role of silence in the blocking of grief resolution and states that this often occurs, '... when a loss is unusual, or a person who has been lost ... [is] ... unknown to the family'. He states that some people, '... feel awkward about expressing their feelings for fear that others will not understand' and that this reluctance to express grief can lead to the person suffering in silence.

Kuhn expands on the issue of silence by saying that it has its roots in, '... the defenses of denial, repression, or suppression'. Because mourners do not feel it is safe to express their grief, '... a cycle of silence ... gets established. Kuhn goes on to describe how a communal silence develops which often happens because the community blames the mourner for having made a bad choice. The communal silence is often interpreted by the mourner as disapproval and this reinforces the sense of shame already felt by the mourner. The result of this silence is that the loss is not dealt with, which can lead to 'depression and other mental disorders'. Kuhn stresses the importance of breaking the silence in order to begin to address, '... the chaos that loss often brings - especially loss that seems atypical and is connected with guilt'. When mothers do attend for post-adoption grief counselling, the issues of shame and guilt often feature in the discussions.

Shawyer puts this very succinctly in *Death By Adoption* when she says, 'Of course everybody knows that if she really loves the child, she will give it away and too late she discovers what 'everybody' actually knew all along but conveniently forgot to share with her - the knowledge that if she had really loved the child she would never have given it up!'. Many original mothers feel betrayed by a society which told them to be unselfish and sign adoption consents because it would be best for their children and then made them feel ashamed of their actions afterwards.

Also writing in *Disenfranchised Grief*, Jane Nichols tackles the issues surrounding perinatal loss and mentions adoption loss. She states that because those around them fail to recognise the extent to which they value their child, original mothers sometimes hold on to their grief more tenaciously than they might otherwise have done.

Many women who attend support groups for original mothers express relief at finally being able to express their feelings to someone who understands. This has been described by one original mother as, 'Like being in Italy and meeting the only other person who speaks English'. Breaking the silence is often the first step towards grief resolution for an original mother. The first revelation of her experience is often followed by an outpouring of emotions, which have been bottled up for many years. Now, in the twenty-first century, some people benefit from sharing experiences and feelings with others via internet sites, although dangers do exist there, especially for the emotionally vulnerable.

Silence has also been used to suppress the grief of adopted people. Many adoptive parents profess to having been quite open with their children about their adoptive status and say that it has never been a secret. While this may be true, in many cases the adoption is announced once and then never discussed again. What kind of message does this send to those who are adopted? They often assume from the behaviour of others that adoption is something not very pleasant, a topic not to be discussed, but to be avoided.

When adoptive parents do not correct visitors who, unaware of the nature of family relationships, claim to see a genetic resemblance between parents and children, the adopted child may form the impression that adoption is something unmentionable and that other people are better left in the dark. Sometimes, sadly, attempts by adopted children to discuss the situation openly are met with disappointment by adoptive parents and thereby discouraged.

Anthropologists have discovered a wide variety of funeral rites throughout the ages and throughout the world and it is clear that many cultures have created a series of activities to assist the bereaved to adjust to their loss. Rituals provide the bereaved with permission to mourn.

In *Disenfranchised Grief*, Vanderlyn Pine discusses Freud's notion that grieving allows the griever to obtain, '... a kind of 'freedom' from the dead person'. Many original mothers feel that because they were not permitted to grieve, they have not been able to achieve that 'freedom' and so their mourning becomes chronic and unresolved. The families and friends of original mothers are often surprised many years later to hear of the pain that they have suffered because their grief at the time was 'apparently absent'. Pine points out that this apparent absence of grief can, in fact, be a sign of acute grief which has been repressed and/or delayed.

Pine states that the purposes of funeral rites include; announcing the death, recognising the place which the dead person held in society, assisting the bereaved through the process of grief, delimiting the period of mourning, allowing the grievers to express their emotions publicly and allowing the members of the community to gather to support each other. Pine comments on the 'pathological reactions to bereavement' caused by 'the absence of understood social expectations and acceptable rituals for mourning'. Often at the funeral, or the wake, friends and family members recall events in the life of the deceased person and discuss his or her personal characteristics. This provides comfort and reassurance to the bereaved. The recollection of happy events can bring a positive note to a sad occasion.

For the original mother, there is generally no formal announcement of the birth or the adoption of her child; in fact the activity often takes place in secret. Her child is not given the opportunity to be granted a place in society as the procedure of adoption denies the child's place in the original family.

Frequently no one assists the original mother through the process of grief, as there is usually no recognition that she has suffered a loss. Because there is no ritual to delimit the period of mourning, many original mothers describe their grief as 'a life sentence'.

Original mothers have no opportunity to express their grief publicly at the time of their loss, as society is embarrassed by their situation and does not grant them acceptance or permission to grieve. There is commonly no gathering of the community around the original mother. Instead she is often shunned and ostracised. There are no happy recollections to comfort her.

Adoption and Loss

There are no recognised rituals to assist original mothers to accept the loss of their children. Original mothers were not even given any document to prove that they had, in fact, given birth. One of the recommendations of the Third Australian Conference on Adoption held in Adelaide in 1982 was that original parents be provided with documentation of the fact of adoption as well as access to original birth certificates at all times. It is now standard practice in South Australia to ensure that the original mother has a copy of the child's birth certificate and a copy of their consent to the adoption.

Adopted people, also, are not given copies of their original birth certificates until they become adults and, in some countries, may then apply for them. This is a denial of the fact that they existed as individuals prior to the adoption process. Many adopted people are not even aware that they have two birth certificates. Some adopted people, as a way of reclaiming their identity, change their names back to the original once they have their original birth certificates. Others, like my son, create a new name and identity for themselves which is neither their original name nor their adoptive name.

Many adopted people feel that because they were infants at the time of the adoption, it was something that was done without their knowledge or consent and therefore experience feelings of anger and powerlessness. There are no recognised rituals for them, as adults, to help them to come to terms with their adoption loss.

Although the lack of ritual is another factor that can prevent adoption separation grief from being resolved, it is possible for personal rituals to be created at any time, as an aid to grief resolution.

Chapter 5 Disenfranchised grief

In his book *Disenfranchised Grief*, Kenneth Doka describes some situations in which resolution of grief does not occur, because the grief is 'disenfranchised' that is, not recognised and supported by the community. He points out that, 'Most of the losses we experience are not due to physical death'. Doka describes feelings of bereaved persons such as anger, guilt, sadness, depression, hopelessness and numbness and states that these reactions can be complicated when grief is disenfranchised. The mourners whose grief is disenfranchised are, by virtue of this, cut off from social supports and so have few opportunities to express and resolve their feelings.

Doka describes disenfranchised grief as grief connected to a loss which cannot be openly acknowledged, publicly mourned or socially supported. He expands on this description by saying that in many cases of disenfranchised grief, either the relationship is not recognised, the loss is not recognised or the griever is not recognised.

Although Doka points out that, '... we are just becoming aware of the sense of loss that people experience in giving children up for adoption' and he acknowledges that, '... significant losses can occur even when the object of the loss remains physically alive', he does not explore further in his book the loss experienced by the original mother of an adopted child. Because the birth by an unmarried mother of an illegitimate child and the

175

subsequent transfer of that child to a legitimate married couple was often shrouded in secrecy, it is obvious that the grief associated with the loss of that child would not have been openly acknowledged, publicly mourned, nor socially supported.

Grief is repressed or delayed when there are no opportunities to perform the grief work. Whereas traditionally mourners would turn to their families for emotional support, because original mothers were often perceived as having brought shame on the family, that avenue of support was likely to be closed to them. Many original mothers report that after the loss of their child, friends and family members either avoided their company or when in their company, avoided any mention of the pregnancy or the lost child. In this way it often appeared to the original mother that those around her were colluding with society to deny her experience and her loss. In fact those people, like the original mother herself, had no previous experience which was comparable to this one on which to draw and were themselves at a loss as to how to react.

The practice of issuing the adopted child with a new birth certificate, which can be interpreted as evidence that the adoptive mother gave birth to the child, allows public denial of the existence of the original mother and therefore of her loss.

In *Disenfranchised Grief*, Jeffrey Kauffman states that when grief is disenfranchised, '... the bereaved may become disillusioned with and alienated from their community' and that this can affect one's sense of identity and belonging. Many original mothers speak of feeling isolated and misunderstood by society in general. Original mothers would not be surprised to hear Kauffman say that, '... loss of community that may occur as a consequence of disenfranchised grief fosters an abiding sense of loneliness and abandonment'. Adopted people often raise issues of their sense of identity and sense of belonging. Because they are told that, by virtue of being adopted, they are 'special', 'chosen' and 'fortunate', their grief at the separation from their original

176

mother is denied, by society and often by their adoptive parents.
If they try to express their feelings of grief they risk being labelled 'ungrateful'.

Doka addresses the subject of 'elective loss' by commenting on the grief associated with abortion. Doka says that women do experience grief when they choose to terminate a pregnancy. This conclusion is partly based on research, which shows the extent of bonding between the expectant mother and her unborn child. Jane Nichols says about perinatal loss that, 'There is often an erroneous assumption that because the relationship between a newly born infant and a parent is one that is expected to exist primarily in the future, that the bonds that are joined throughout pregnancy are thus negated or non-existent. Those who hold these attitudes are apt, then, to be unresponsive toward both the loss and the grieving parents'.

The grief of original mothers has been disenfranchised for several reasons and in several ways. In some cases the pregnancy and birth of the child were kept totally secret because of the shame involved and so the original mother had no choice but to conceal her grief also. In many cases, original mothers were told by family members, by friends, by religious groups, that they were 'doing the right thing'. This, in fact, constitutes a denial of the legitimacy of their grief and so they often felt guilty and ashamed and thought that their grief was caused by selfishness or self-pity.

The result of this denial of their feelings was often a deepening of those feelings. Many original mothers will agree with Meagher that, '... denial does not cause feelings to disappear, in fact they grow in intensity'. Kauffman states that, '... the specific psychological phenomenon operating in disenfranchised grief is shame'. When adopted people grow up in a family where the adoption is not referred to, they sense a feeling of shame attached to adoption. This is more intense if the adoption is actually concealed from the adopted person until they are an adult. Kauffman discusses the memory of past unsanctioned grief. He states that it does not evaporate over time. Kauffman also points out that, '... when a new loss occurs, the old disenfranchisement will affect the new situation, and may enforce a repetition of the earlier inhibited grief pattern'. He also confirms that a new bereavement can cause a previous disenfranchised grief to emerge.

Vanderlyn Pine points out that, '... the presence of disenfranchised grief can easily complicate and compromise many other situations'. Because they have often concealed their grief in order to be compliant in their adoptive families and because they may have rejected intimacy through fear of abandonment, adopted people often appear cool and lacking in emotional attachment. Getting in touch with their feelings of grief and sharing them can help them to relate better to other people.

Shame is a word used by many original mothers to describe their feelings at the time of their pregnancy and at the time of separation from their children. The number of adoptions in South Australia gradually increased from the introduction of the Adoption Act in 1925 until 1972, when the number of adoptions began to reduce. During this period society regarded being single and pregnant as a shameful condition.

Adoption was seen as the solution to what society viewed as a problem. Through adoption it was thought that the unmarried mother would be rescued from her shameful state and the child would be rescued from the shameful condition of illegitimacy. Because of society's condemnation, single, pregnant women were disempowered and manipulated by a paternalistic social structure.

Many original mothers found, however, that far from feeling rescued, they ultimately felt ashamed of not having been able to prevent their child from being adopted. It is no wonder that they found it impossible to confront their grief as their feelings of shame made them believe that their grief was not legitimate. Many allowed their shame to prevent them from sharing their grief with others. Kauffman states that shame can lead to a fear of abandonment. Original mothers often describe how for them the risk of abandonment was too great to allow them to share their grief with anyone. As a result of their fears their sadness grew secretly within them. Original mothers have spent many years hiding the fact that they had lost a child through adoption, as they feared that they would lose the approval of friends and family members if their secret became known.

The lack of community recognition is yet another factor that blocks the resolution of adoption-related grief.

Chapter 6 Grief Resolution?

Resolution, or acceptance, is considered by many of those who write about grief counselling to be the desired outcome of mourning. Pine describes resolution of grief as the point at which the pain can be accepted and 'lived with', ie the griever, '... feels that life can continue without the one who has died'.

Reaching a position of resolution for mothers who have no information about the children from whom they have been separated by adoption is extremely difficult and perhaps impossible. In some ways they are in a position similar to those whose loved ones are 'missing in action' during wartime. When hostilities are over there are always those whose fate is uncertain and there are always those who mourn them, never knowing whether or not their loved ones will return. Resolution is therefore denied them.

Many original mothers describe similar feelings of always wondering whether or not their child is still alive and whether or not their child will want to see them again. They live with this uncertainty, some of them for the rest of their lives and so their grief can remain unresolved and their mourning may become chronic.

Kate Inglis presented a paper at the Third Australian Adoption Conference in 1982, in which she stated that for the original mother this, '... acceptance that appears essential to the theories of resolution of grief is ... fraught with difficulties'. The

The Hidden Grief

difficulty illustrated by Inglis is that of deciding what it is that the original mother must accept.

In her paper, Inglis describes the predicament of the original mother very movingly:

Which particular thing is she to accept ... that she has a child who is lost to her but not dead; that she was responsible for its loss on the day she surrendered the legal rights and obligations of parenthood; that she lives in a world in which some mothers are rewarded and others punished for their fertility; that most people failed her, that she failed herself; that she did the right thing; that she did the wrong thing; that she grieves, that grief is not appropriate; that she is unnatural in her ability to take such a course; that she is natural in thinking of her baby before herself or conversely of thinking of herself before the baby; that she was, and still is, isolated in her experience; that her grief cannot be resolved and must somehow be lived with alone? What is she to accept to reach the tranquillity glowingly described as following acceptance in the most commonly used grief theory model. Must she also now accept another failure, ie to successfully deal with her grief?

Because of the unique nature of the loss experienced by original mothers, as outlined above, professionals who are entrusted with the care of these women should be aware of their particular issues and of the fact that the traditional methods of grief counselling will not be appropriate for original mothers. Their unique experience of loss demands a unique approach.

The experience of the woman who has lost a child through adoption means that her grief cannot be resolved in the same way that the grief associated with other losses can be resolved. Can it, in fact, be resolved?

When I first attended ARMS as a client in 1989, I began a course of what was then known as 'Post Relinquishment Grief Counselling', which was provided by Meg Hale, the first social worker to be employed by ARMS. This counselling programme had been designed specifically for mothers who had been separated from their children by adoption. When I later gained my social work qualification and was myself employed by ARMS to provide Post Relinquishment Grief Counselling, I created my own version of it, based on the material presented in the original version of this book.

In 2006, after I had resigned from my employment with ARMS, the South Australian Government set up the Post Adoption Support Services (PASS), which offers post-adoption support and counselling by professional staff to anyone whose life has been affected by adoption separation. PASS is operated by an independent community organisation called Relationships Australia and is fully funded by the government of South Australia, which means that there is no cost to clients for their services. South Australians are very fortunate to have this excellent service available to them at no cost, as part of the state government's commitment to supporting and assisting those who have experienced adoption separation.

At the time that they were separated from their children, original mothers were denied all of the components of grief work generally recommended by those in the field of grief counselling. They had no rituals to assist the grief process. They were unable to achieve resolution because of the absence of finality involved in their loss. They were denied social supports. They had no opportunities to express their grief. Their grief was often seriously affected by their feelings of guilt and shame. Can the mistakes of the past be somehow undone? Can original mothers somehow experience at a later time the components of grief, which were missing from their lives at the time of their loss?

The first and most important factor for original mothers is to break the silence which, in many cases, has crippled them emotionally since the loss of their children. For many mothers, breaking their silence about their lost children happens in the safety of a support group. A support group is commonly understood to be a group of people with common experiences and concerns who provide emotional and moral support for one another. Knowing that all of them have shared a common experience enables the members of the group to feel safe and comfortable.

Many valuable and successful support groups operate for original mothers and for those who are adopted. Not only can they provide a safe, supportive environment for their members, but they also play an important part in educating the general public and also politicians. Support groups have been influential in persuading politicians to pass important legislation in relation to adoption. Those who attend support groups often gain confidence from each other and benefit from observing each other's growth.

For most original mothers, the relief of breaking the silence is cathartic. It is very empowering and brings with it a flood of relief. Living with such a secret usually creates a huge mental and emotional strain and the original mother who has become used to living this way will feel a great weight lifted from her shoulders. Sharing one's experience in a supportive environment can be a way of replacing the ritual that was not available to either mother or child at the time of separation.

The truth is that being a mother who has been separated from her child by adoption is *a permanent condition*. The mother who finds herself in this position can expect to be reminded of her condition frequently, in her conversations and relationships with others.

There are certainly ways of understanding and acknowledging her experience, which can improve her well-being, but she will always be conscious of the fact that although the past can be accepted and understood, it cannot be undone. All those whose lives have been affected by adoption separation can benefit from creating their own methods of self-care and from sharing their feelings with others who understand.

Adoption and Loss

Obtaining a copy of the original birth certificate can be a part of creating ritual. The original mother should be entitled to have this document because it represents her experience of giving birth. It verifies what society has denied, that the adopted child is indeed her child. When she signed the adoption consent form, she lost her right to be the legal parent of that child. She did not give up the right to love her child, to care about her child's future or to have a relationship with her child.

For the adopted person, having their original birth certificate in their possession confirms for them that they did exist prior to the adoption and gives a sense of reality to that existence. Obtaining their original birth certificate can be the first step in understanding who they are and in uniting the two aspects of their identity.

With the passage of time and the changes that have occurred in society, there has come an increased understanding in the community around the long term impact of adoption separation. This has happened because many family members who had been separated by adoption have chosen to make their experiences and their feelings known publicly, in order to educate the community about adoption separation, how it happened and its long term impact. Secrecy has been damaging to all of the parties to adoption. The legislators who sanctioned adoptions, the professionals who enacted adoption legislation, the adopters, the original parents, family members and friends who supported the notion that the original mother should not raise her child; all have to live with the results of their actions.

Increased community awareness of adoption separation issues will allow those affected to address their losses without fear of criticism. The apologies which have taken place in Australia have made a huge contribution to bringing adoption issues to the attention of the general population and alleviating some of the distress felt by those who have been separated from family members by adoption. The funding of post-adoption services by both state and federal governments is further acknowledgment of the special needs of those whose lives have been affected by past adoptions. These services not only provide support and counselling for those who wish to address loss and grief issues connected to adoption separation, they also provide support and information should clients wish to try to make contact with a family member from whom they have been separated by adoption.

Chapter 7 Reunion

At the Sixth Australian Conference on Adoption, in Brisbane in 1997, Sarah Berryman reported on research into adoption reunions and their effects on people's lives which had been undertaken at a post adoption centre in New South Wales. The researchers interviewed eighty-one people who had used the centre to mediate on their behalf. They found that a majority of 'searchers' and, interestingly, an even larger majority of 'found' people described the reunion relationship in entirely positive or in largely positive terms and that although 59% of those who had been found reported that they had not planned to search for family members, eighty of the eighty-one people interviewed had no regrets about the reunion.

There is no doubt that contact between family members who have been separated by adoption is a very important contributing factor to the resolution of their grief. For those original mothers and adopted people who never experience a reunion, however, there are ways of confronting and easing their pain. Some are able to express their feelings in art or literature and some find satisfaction in supporting others in similar situations.

For many people whose lives have been affected by adoption separation, there never comes a time when they feel that they have finally 'resolved' those issues. Grief resolution is a process and while generally progress can be assessed over one's

The Hidden Grief

life, there will be times in which it feels easier to come to terms with one's experience and other times when it will be more of a challenge.

Reunion and mothers

At the time that their children were adopted, some mothers were told to forget about them. In my experience, this very rarely happened. I did work with one mother who had been raised in a very isolated area. She was sexually assaulted when she was under age and was not even aware that she was pregnant. Arrangements were made for her to go to hospital and the neighbours were told that she had a 'stomach problem'. The baby was delivered under a general anaesthetic and she was discharged and taken home to recover. Many years later she was contacted by her son. When he told her that he believed she was his mother, she said that she was very sorry to disappoint him, but she had never had any children. He persisted and produced a hospital form with her signature on it. She was amazed and they agreed to have blood tests to solve the mystery. She was indeed his mother and she was so happy to have a son. He was equally happy to have found his mother. Such cases, of course, are very rare.

In the vast majority of cases, mothers who have been separated from their children by adoption are all too aware that their child is probably still alive somewhere in the world. Most mothers would like to know what became of their child, although some fear hearing bad news, which would add to their distress at the separation from their child. Others, who have not felt able or ready to share the fact that they had given birth to a child who was raised in another family, may live in fear of their secret being exposed.

However, there are many mothers who wait anxiously for their children to become adults so that they can try to find them. Having access to the adoption records of their adult children is not an unusual expectation for mothers. After all, when the adoption took place, they lost the right to parent their children. Parental rights and responsibilities end when the child legally becomes an adult; in most countries now this occurs by the age of eighteen. Parents who have the opportunity to raise their children are generally unable to make decisions on their behalf once they reach the age of legal adulthood.

The state should be no different; the state also should have no right to restrict information on behalf of people who are legally adults. A mother who wishes to contact her adult child is one adult relating to another adult. There is no other situation in which an adult can be prevented from knowing the identity or whereabouts of another adult when no law has been broken and there is no evidence that there is a potential risk or danger involved.

There is no justification for denying original parents information regarding the identities and whereabouts of their adult children, just because they were prevented from raising those children to adulthood. Original parents, however, often do not receive support from the community when they wish to find their lost children. As Shawyer says in *Death by Adoption*, 'If she should try to trace the child ... she is cruelly reminded that she has served her function and that really society couldn't care less what happens to her now'.

In most Western countries, in the middle of the twentieth century when so many adoptions occurred, they were based on secrecy. Information was legally sealed and, in some countries, the long term plan was that neither those who were adopted nor their original parents would ever have access to each other's identities.

There have been changes to adoption laws in recent years in many Australian states. South Australia led the way in 1989 by being the first Australian state to give mothers and adopted adults equal rights to access identifying information about each other,

The Hidden Grief

when the adopted person reached adulthood. This move was consistent with South Australia's long-standing commitment to women's rights. South Australia was the first place in the world to give women the right to stand for Parliament, in 1894 and the second place (after New Zealand in 1893) to give women the right to vote.

As a result of the availability of adoption information, many family members who have been separated by adoption in South Australia are able to be reunited. These changes came about at the request of those whose lives had been affected by adoption separation. The changes to the Adoption Act reflected a change in community perceptions about adoption. Adoption is no longer viewed as a one-off event which is completed with the court order. There is now more recognition that it is a healthy emotional reaction for adopted people to seek contact with their original families and for original parents to wish to know the children from whom they have been separated.

There have also been changes in recent years to adoption legislation in the United Kingdom. In Scotland, adopted people have had access to their original birth certificates, at the age of seventeen, since adoption legislation came into effect in 1930. In England and Wales, adopted people have only had access to their original birth certificates since 1975. In neither country, sadly, do brothers and sisters of adopted people have any right to information about their lost siblings.

Original parents in the United Kingdom also have no legal right to access information about their adult adopted children. In contrast, I, like many others in the United Kingdom, have spent many happy hours researching my family history and have had access to records of my ancestors going back hundreds of years. I have read records of many births, marriages and deaths, yet information about the adoption of my own son is not available to me.

Adoption and Loss

There is no reason why adoption information should be any different from other official records. Adoption is a legal arrangement like a marriage; there is no excuse for keeping it a secret once the adopted person is an adult. I seriously hope that one day, in the not too distant future, legislators in all countries will recognise and understand the issues for family members separated by adoption and change the legislation to allow fair and equal access to adoption information.

I encourage every mother to search for her child, without reservation. The search itself is empowering as it validates her identity as the mother of her child and allows her to declare that she cares about her child. One of the barriers to grief resolution for mothers is the lack of finality, their total ignorance of what became of their children. By finding their lost children, mothers are giving those children a great opportunity; the opportunity to know not only their mothers, but also their families and their history. This can only lead to adopted people knowing themselves even better.

When an adoption has taken place, the original mother and the adopted person are both living with loss and ignorance. For adopted people as well as for mothers it is emotionally healthier to confront the truth than to live a half-life of fantasy or fear. Reality can be therapeutic.

The original mother has always been present in her child and so, in a sense, she has always been present in her child's life. She has simply been waiting until she can be acknowledged. Inviting her adult child to acknowledge her allows that adult child to make an informed choice.

Family members who have been separated by adoption are not 'strangers' to each other. The relationship between those who are closely related and those who are genuinely strangers is quite different. Strangers do not search for similarities in each other's physical appearance, personality, or life events, because they have no reason to expect that these will exist.

The Hidden Grief

Many mothers have spent a large part of their lives apologising and sometimes it is difficult for them to stop. They apologised for having a sexual relationship before they were married, they apologised for being pregnant, they apologised for not having been able to prevent the adoption of their children and they apologised for not being able to forget their children.

There is no need to apologise to anyone for wanting to find your lost child. It is a perfectly legitimate activity. How else are they ever going to know that their mothers care about them?

Some mothers fear that their child may not know of the adoption. If adoptive parents have chosen to deceive their adopted child, then they know from the outset that they risk being exposed one day and that this exposure can only harm their relationship with that child. There is nothing to be gained by supporting this cruel deception. Parents can only help their children by releasing them from deceit.

For all of those who decide to search for family from whom they have been separated, careful preparation is advised. I strongly recommend to people preparing for a reunion that they read, talk and think a great deal before the event. It is particularly useful to talk to people who have already experienced a reunion.

Family members who have been separated often want to know each other. If they have undertaken relevant preparation before contact with the other party, they will understand that many people have been deeply affected by adoption separation. Many lies have been told and many feelings have been suppressed.

Healing the pain can be a long, slow process and it is impossible to know before contact what stage the other person has reached. Some are not at a place in their lives where they are able even to start the healing process and are not ready for contact. This is another example of the damage that has been caused by adoption, but patience and understanding will hopefully pay off in the long run. After all, there are tensions and differences in families that have always lived together. There is always the potential for disharmony when the family is coming together again after a long separation. There are also new people to meet; there are stories to tell, feelings to share and adjustments to be made. These adjustments can take time. It is wise to be prepared for any eventuality.

If there are problems in relationships after family members who have been separated by adoption are reunited, the problems are caused by the original separation, not by the reunion. Problems will exist whether reunion takes place or not. It is adoption, not reunion, which causes the problems in the first place. It is not the truth that hurts people involved with adoption; it is the lies and ignorance that have gone before.

Unfortunately, in some countries, those who create adoption legislation do not comprehend this or prefer not to confront it. It is morally insupportable that original parents and adopted people are still not allowed access to information about each other in some parts of the world. Family members who have been separated by adoption often want to be reunited and if the legislation in their part of the world does not support them to do this, they often find other methods of locating each other, such as accessing internet sites, which may not lead to a positive outcome.

Most people support the rights of adopted people to know their history, but mothers also have a moral right to search for their children. If a child is kidnapped, taken by force, we expect the parents to do everything in their power to find their lost child. *Our children were also taken from us by force*, not always by physical force, but also by the force of public opinion.

After losing their children, many mothers experienced feelings of numbness, emptiness, sadness, a sense of unreality and a sense of loss. They may have been told that they should be 'getting over it' and 'getting on with their lives' and 'putting it behind them'. Many of them felt guilty and apologetic about their feelings and so did not share them with anyone. We understand now, many years later, that they had experienced a significant

192

emotional upheaval and had suffered a major loss and that their feelings were, in fact, the natural reaction to what they had experienced.

Some of them have been fortunate enough to be reunited with their lost children. People love to hear reunion stories and talk about 'happy endings', as if the reunion itself solved everything and made it all right again. We know now that it does not. The reunion itself is another major emotional experience and for many mothers brings back the feelings of emptiness, loss and sadness that they felt when they were first separated from their children. Again, people may be telling them that they should be happy and looking to the future and not the past and they are often made to feel guilty and apologetic yet again for still having those painful feelings even after they have met their children again.

Psychologists tell us that it takes from two to five years to recover from a major emotional upheaval. It was difficult for mothers to recover from the loss of their children because their grief at the time was not recognised and therefore was not addressed. Finding their lost children again is another major emotional upheaval. Meeting their children again will often bring strong emotions to the surface. Those feelings are just as natural as the feelings they had after their children were adopted.

Once they can accept that their feelings are legitimate, they can then begin to address them. There is no need for mothers to feel guilty or inadequate because they are still suffering, even after they have found their children again. Mothers need just as much support after meeting their children again as they did after losing their children in the first place.

Reunion and adopted people

I encourage adopted people also, without reservation, to search for their original parents. Many professionals, psychologists and social workers now understand that for an adopted person to search for his or her original families and background is a healthy, legitimate response to being raised apart from them. This may not have been clear in the middle of the twentieth century. At that time many adoptive parents believed that as the children they were adopting would have no conscious memories of their families of origin, they would have no interest in pursuing any kind of relationship with them. Many now understand, however, that a reunion with the original families is something that can be not only expected but also actively encouraged. Lifton says, in *Journey of the Adopted Self* that 'Healing begins when adoptees take control of their lives by making the decision to search'.

Shawyer points out, in *Death by Adoption*, however, that some members of the community are less understanding. She says, 'People who are not adopted spend money and time trekking the world in search of their ancestral heritage ... Family trees are pored over ... by people who know who they are...We don't think that's strange or unhealthy, and yet adopted people ... mount the same intensive ... search, and are treated unsympathetically, even cruelly for their efforts'.

We are all a combination of genetics and environment. When they acknowledge and embrace their origins, adults who were adopted as children are accepting themselves as whole people, made up of three families, the two families into which they were born and the family within which they were raised.

Adults who were adopted as children can be supported to search for members of their original families and hopefully build relationships with them. They can be supported in looking for what those of us who were not adopted take for granted; their inheritance, their history, their family members and their forebears. Searching for their original families can be made easy for adopted people, in many ways. It can be made easy by legislation, which recognises their situation and their identity issues. It can be made easy emotionally by a positive attitude in their adoptive families and in the community in general and by the recognition that searching for their families of origin is a healthy, positive step in their development. Having more people in your life who care about you can only be an advantage.

Lifton talks about the lack of understanding among adoptive parents and in the community of the desire that adopted people have to communicate with their original mothers. She says, 'Those who know their mothers cannot imagine what it is like not to know the woman who brought you into the world'. Adopted people who search for their original families are a credit to the way their adoptive parents have raised them and I know that many adoptive parents are proud of their adopted children who have built relationships with their original families.

Because of the fear of their adoptive parents' reactions, some adopted people postpone the search for their original families until after the deaths of their adoptive parents. This suggests that they believe that their adoptive parents would not be happy for them to find wholeness and healing. If they postpone the search for their original families until after the deaths of their adoptive parents, adopted people are denying their adoptive parents an opportunity for growth and the possibility of sharing that important experience with their adopted children.

Many times, when adopted people have postponed their search for this reason, they have found that they have left it too late and that their original parents are dead also. A sad example of this is the story of Ingrid Pedersen, the half-sister of singer/songwriter John Lennon.

In 2005, Ms Pedersen (under the name of Ingrid Pederson Lennon) produced a book in French, entitled *Mon frère s'appelait John Lennon* (*My brother's name was John Lennon*). The book was written in collaboration with Judith Carraz. Ingrid Pedersen was born four years after her famous brother and was separated from the family through adoption. John Lennon learned of her existence in 1964 and spent the next sixteen years, until his untimely death, desperately trying to find her.

Adoption and Loss

Under English adoption legislation, however, he had no legal right to information about his sister and so he was not successful. Ms Pedersen chose to wait until the death of her adoptive mother in 1998 to begin her search for her family of origin. By this time, not only was her original mother already dead, but her famous half-brother also.

Adopted people who search for their original parents and families would be wise to do so with an open mind and with a genuine willingness to accept the outcome. Some adopted people find that their original mothers have suffered greatly from having lost them. They may then mistakenly assume that, by being adopted, they have been spared the experience of being raised by a mother who went on to experience such difficulties, not realising that it could well have been the loss of her child which had led to her suffering. Some mothers have even died through suicide before being able to be reunited with their children. This is a particularly sad circumstance, as it is possible that had they been reunited with their children, the suicide may well not have taken place.

Robert Dessaix is an adopted person and the author of a book entitled *A Mother's Disgrace*, published in 1994. Dessaix is also a successful broadcaster and has written several books on other topics, which have been highly praised. *A Mother's Disgrace* is an absorbing and moving account of his search for his family of origin.

Dessaix was born in 1944 in Melbourne, Australia, adopted as an infant and raised as an only child. He knew from an early age that his original mother's surname was Dessaix and wove fantasies of noble ancestors. He was raised with the surname of Jones but reverted to using the name of Dessaix after the deaths of his adoptive parents.

His book is not a linear account, but a swirl of events and connections, which sometimes feels like a literary 'join-the-dots'. His story includes his interest in all things Russian, his growing

The Hidden Grief

awareness of his sexuality, travel to interesting and exotic parts of the world and the search for his origins.

Dessaix describes how when he was very young, he created in his mind a 'parallel world' in order to give himself a history that he 'had some control over'. This is a common thread in the narratives of adopted people. Because the adoption took place without their knowledge or consent, they sometimes feel that they grow up with a feeling of powerlessness over their own fate (in spite of the fact that those of us who were not adopted also had no say in what happened during our infancy).

For example, in *Journey of the Adopted Self*, Lifton says of adopted people; 'Much of their imagery is not centred in the adoptive family ... but rather in fantasy and imagination'.

Of his adoptive mother, Dessaix says that she loved him, '... as a kind of exotic plant she'd promised faithfully to tend'. His mother had had a nervous breakdown before they adopted him and he was always afraid that if, '... [he] were not very good, it might happen again'.

Finally, as an adult, Dessaix met, in a strange coincidence, a woman who shared exactly the same name as his original mother, Yvonne Dessaix. He calls her 'Yvonne-not-my-mother'. She did lead him, however, to the woman who was his original mother. Dessaix makes it clear that the reason he decided to try to locate his original mother was not unhappiness. He says, 'I'd never have taken the step I next took if I'd been unhappy'. He describes himself at the time as being content with his life and says that he, '... would not have contacted her if [he] had not been content'.

Many adopted people also search for their original families at a time of contentment. It is quite wrong of people to assume that the search necessarily is associated with some sort of crisis in the adopted person's life.

Dessaix made the contact with his original mother through the other Yvonne Dessaix, who forwarded a letter from him. A few days later his mother wrote to him and he rang her. He describes

197

their first conversation over the telephone as taking place 'tentatively, shyly, happily'. They then arranged to meet.

As he walked towards her, he says that his mother 'smiled a smile of boundless hurt and happiness' and that they both wanted to 'say nothing and everything all at once'. Dessaix's mother tells him how she was afraid he would feel bitter, because she had 'abandoned' him. He is confused. He considers her 'blameless'.

Dessaix refers frequently in the book to his difficulties with the fact that his mother had been raised with and accepted unquestioningly, a value system which was quite foreign to him. He found it hard to understand her notion that she had acted immorally by being sexually active outside of marriage. He therefore found it difficult to accept her feelings of shame connected to his birth.

Between the time he was born in 1944 and the time he was reunited with his mother, in 1989, there had been a huge shift in what was considered socially and morally acceptable behaviour. He finds it hard to comprehend the degree of shame and disgrace attached to his mother's behaviour and seems surprised by the fact that his existence was never ('never ... ever, under any circumstances') referred to within her family for forty-six years, until his original mother told his grandmother that they had had contact.

He describes the lines of guilt and blame that he found to be 'so insidious, so intricate, someone of my generation can barely disentangle them'.

At the end of their first meeting Dessaix describes his feelings: '... a rush of affection, of thankfulness to this woman for being what she was, of completeness at last - no, not completeness, but completion, of weaving two parts together to make a whole'. He says that he and his mother started their new relationship together, '... with deep, generous liking and thankfulness that the silence had been broken'.

The Hidden Grief

As their relationship develops, his mother tells him that her sense of grief 'never goes away' and he grows to have a deeper understanding of the impact on her life of having been pressured by her family to give him up for adoption. This understanding leads him to profess, '... a regret I can scarcely measure for what happened to Yvonne'.

The feelings expressed by Robert Dessaix are common among adopted people. The desire to connect with the families of origin is often very strong and when a feeling of peace and wholeness is achieved by the reunion, it can be very powerful.

There is still much that could be learned about the effects of adoption on the lives of adopted people. Accounts such as this one have made a significant contribution to the understanding in the community of the benefits to adopted people of connecting with their original families.

Reunion and adoptive parents

To ensure that the title of this section is not misleading, I should like to make it clear that the use of the word *reunion* refers to a meeting between family members who have been separated by adoption. Adoptive parents have not been separated from a family member by adoption and so they do not experience adoption reunions. However, support and understanding from adoptive parents can make the reunion experience more meaningful and comfortable for those involved.

In Australia, family members who have been separated by adoption have a legal right to apply to access identifying information about each other, once the adopted person is an adult.

When seeking to contact an adult who was adopted as a child, therefore, it is not appropriate to contact that person's adoptive parents. Taking such a step actually robs the adopted person of the autonomy to which they are entitled, as an adult, to respond to a reunion invitation in the way that they choose.

Adoption and Loss

All parents have an obligation to their children to provide the best possible environment in which they can grow and develop. Some adopted people feel that being unaware of their background puts them at a disadvantage, because important parts of their history and identity are missing.

Some adoptive parents say that when they adopted they expected never to hear from the original parents of the child again. They complain that changes to legislation, which have made adoption information available, are unfair. The reality is that there are few certainties in life. Some changes we have to learn to accept, especially when they are changes for the better. Unrealistic assurances from social workers do not make lying and hiding the truth the right thing to do.

Regardless of legislation, many family members separated by adoption have been able to find each other over the years and whether or not adoption information is available as a legal right, it has always been a moral right. Inadequacies in the legal system do not excuse efforts being made to keep family members apart.

In fact, governments frequently change laws, especially when society becomes aware of inequities. Those whose lives have been affected by adoption separation have been able to bring about changes to inequitable and discriminatory legislation by speaking out.

In *Death by Adoption*, Joss Shawyer tells the story of Brenda, an Australian woman, living in New Zealand, who adopted two Maori girls, named Ann and Josie. Brenda came to realise the injustice of the girls being separated from their original families and began to search for the girls' original mothers when Josie was nine and Ann was twelve.

Brenda believed that a reunion between her adopted daughters and their respective original mothers would be to the advantage of all concerned.

At the time the book was written, Brenda had not yet found Ann's mother. Brenda did find Josie's mother, however and

The Hidden Grief

arranged to meet her by herself, before suggesting a meeting with Josie. Josie discovered that she had twin brothers who were full brothers. When Brenda saw Josie with her original mother and brothers, she said, 'I felt that they belonged together and should never have been separated. I'm sure she could fit into their lives and I could accept it as being right'. Josie's original mother expressed the hope to Brenda that they, '... could perhaps ... do things together as families instead of splitting her from you or splitting her from me'.

It seems that both mothers understood that they each had a close connection to Josie and that neither of them owned her. Brenda says that the experience of reuniting her adopted daughter with her family of origin forced her to look things 'right in the eye' which she previously 'hadn't thought too closely about'. Regarding the future of this relationship, Brenda expressed the opinion that, 'things will only get better'.

Brenda goes on to describe how she began to understand the feelings of the original mother and came to the conclusion that adoption is 'wrong in most cases'. Brenda says that when she adopted her daughters she was told that the original mothers had given them up voluntarily. This notion, of course, made it easier for her to accept the children and the adoptions. She says that at the time of the adoptions she did not want to think about the original mother and 'the heartaches she went through'.

Brenda says that the experience of reuniting Josie with her family of origin has made her a 'better, more honest person'. She now feels 'dreadfully sorry for the mothers' and believes that separating them from their children with no communication between the two is 'dreadful' and 'cruel'.

Brenda says, 'Adoptive parents who aren't honest with themselves must have lots of guilty consciences' and '.I honestly feel now that if you love a child enough, then you can't possibly lose them'. Brenda adds, '... I feel now that they're borrowed, and the sooner they know their natural family the better'.

Adoption and Loss

Adoptive parents like Brenda set a wonderful example for other adoptive parents. Brenda adopted her children in the middle of the twentieth century, at a time when there was no expectation that there would ever be any further contact with the families of the children she had adopted. Her experience indicates that, in spite of the fact that such contact was not supported by either legislation or the attitudes prevalent in society at the time, there has always been the option for adoptive parents to seek out the relatives of the children they had adopted.

Sadly, many adoptive parents try to ignore the implications of the fact that they are raising someone else's child and choose not to confront the fact that the child has three families. Brenda, however, ensured that her adopted daughter and her original mother at least had the opportunity to know each other. She felt secure enough in her parenting role to recognise what her adopted child had to gain from knowing her family of origin and made strenuous efforts to bring about that contact.

The Hidden Grief

{This article was first published in the *Australian Journal of Adoption, Vol 7, No 1 (2013)*.
© Evelyn Robinson, 2013}

The Australian Adoption Apology

Australia is the only country in which the government has issued a formal apology for the past adoption policies and practices that had led to so many family separations. This apology, which took place in 2013, was a result of the efforts of many people who had experienced adoption separation, who worked tirelessly over several decades, individually and in groups, to educate the Australian community in general and politicians in particular about their issues. Historically, in Australia, adoption had been seen as a positive outcome for all concerned. Since the early 1980s, however, a movement to acknowledge the grief and loss associated with separating children from their families has grown. This movement culminated in the apologies of the twenty-first century.

The journey to the National Apology for Forced Adoptions began with a recognition of the long term issues for Aboriginal people who had suffered because of past colonialist policies which led to the removal of Aboriginal children from their families and communities. In 1981 the Department of Aboriginal Affairs in New South Wales produced a paper, written by Historian Peter Read, entitled: '*The Stolen Generations – The removal of Aboriginal children in New South Wales 1883 to 1969'*. This paper described the policies and practices which led to the forcible removal of Aboriginal and Torres Strait Islander children from their families by federal, state and territory government agencies as well as church missions. These children

Adoption and Loss

were either adopted into non-Aboriginal families or placed in institutions.

Paul Keating, who became Prime Minister in 1991, delivered a speech the following year at Redfern Park, in which he acknowledged that the actions of the European settlers had caused long term issues of loss and grief for Aboriginal Australians. Following this speech, a campaign gradually gained momentum across Australia, which resulted in pressure being applied to the federal government to investigate this issue further and expose the truth about the long term outcomes for those families which were affected by these past policies and practices. On the 11th of May, 1995, an inquiry was established by the Federal Attorney-General, Michael Lavarch.

The inquiry was completed over the next two years and the report was tabled in the Australian Federal Parliament on the 26th of May, 1997. It was entitled: *'Report of the National Inquiry into the Separation of Aboriginal and Torres Strait Islander Children from Their Families'*, and became known as the *'Bringing Them Home'* report. Its principal aim was 'to trace the past laws, practices and policies which resulted in the separation of Aboriginal and Torres Strait Islander children from their families by compulsion, duress or undue influence, and the effects of those laws, practices and policies'. One year later, the first annual National Sorry Day was held.

In his parliamentary response to the *'Bringing Them Home'* report, the Opposition Leader, Kim Beazley, called for John Howard, who had become Prime Minister in 1996, to make a formal apology on behalf of the Australian people to the Aboriginal and Torres Strait Islander people who had suffered the long term consequences of those past policies and practices. Mr Howard refused to issue an apology. However federal funding was allocated at that time, to help fund counselling, parenting support, family reunion services and an oral history project.

The Hidden Grief

A letter, written by me, in response to Mr Beazley's comments, was published in the South Australian *Sunday Mail*, on the 8th of June, 1997. The letter read as follows:

Like Kim Beazley, I, too, weep for the Aboriginal children who were taken from their families. And I also weep for the parents of those children who will grieve their loss for the rest of their lives. But I also grieve for myself and the thousands of other mothers and fathers like me, whose children were taken from us to be adopted, because it was 'for their own good'. We also expect to grieve the loss of our children for the rest of our lives. In the case of Aboriginal families, their 'sin' in the eyes of society was simply to be Aboriginal. Growing up in an Aboriginal family was considered to be such a disadvantage the children had to be removed for their own protection. In our case, our 'sin' was simply to be single and pregnant. Growing up in a single parent family was seen as such a disadvantage our children had to be taken from us to be adopted by married couples. Does anyone weep for our children? Can we expect an apology?

Between 1997 and 2001, all Australian states and territories apologised to the Stolen Generations. The publicity which surrounded the '*Bringing Them Home*' report and the possibility of a federal apology had a major impact on members of the non-Aboriginal community around Australia, who had experienced adoption separation. Many of those people were aware that their issues were similar in some respects to the outcomes for the Stolen Generations and so efforts were increased to bring those issues to the attention of both politicians and the Australian community.

Kevin Rudd, who became Prime Minster in 2007, finally apologised, on the 13th of February, 2008, on behalf of the Parliament of Australia, to the Stolen Generations of Aboriginal people for the policies and practices of the past. The apology included a resolve 'that the injustices of the past must never, never happen again'.

Then, on the 16th of November, 2009, Prime Minister Kevin Rudd apologised to the Forgotten Australians (ie those who had been raised in care) and the Former British Child Migrants, who had been brought to Australia as children. The apology was for what they had suffered, not only, for many of them, in terms of abuse, but, also for the loss of family, the loss of identity and, in the case of child migrants, the loss of their country. The apology included a commitment to fund appropriate services and supports to those affected. Many of the states and territories also apologised.

One of the reasons given by former Prime Minister John Howard for his refusal to apologise to the Stolen Generations of Aboriginal people was his view that one generation cannot accept responsibility for the actions of an earlier generation. By the end of 2009, however, the Australian people had generally come to accept that there is value in acknowledging the errors of the past and their long term outcomes in the lives of those who have been adversely affected and in putting in place supports and services to assist those affected. From this time forward, those whose lives had been affected by adoption separation stepped up their efforts to bring their issues to the attention of governments.

The first significant step in the journey towards a National Apology for Forced Adoptions took place when the state of Western Australia, on the 19th of October, 2010, became the first state, not only in Australia, but in the world, to apologise to family members separated by adoption for the policies and practices of the past which had led to those separations.

After this apology, the Senate Community Affairs Committee commenced an inquiry into the practice of forcible adoption in Australia between the 1940s and 1980s. The report on this inquiry, entitled '*Commonwealth Contribution to Former Forced Adoption Policies and Practices*' was completed in

The Hidden Grief

February 2012. It was clear from this Senate Inquiry Report that many of those who were adopted were, like the Stolen Generations, removed from their families 'by compulsion, duress or undue influence'. In response to the report, all of the other states and territories in Australia, with the exception of the Northern Territory, issued apologies in 2012 for past adoption separations. The first was South Australia, on the 18th of July, followed by the Australian Capital Territory on the 14th of August, then New South Wales on the 20th of September, Tasmania on the 18th of October, Victoria on the 25th of October and Queensland on the 27th of November.

One of the recommendations of the Senate Inquiry Report was that the Federal Government offer an apology for past adoption policies and practices. Julia Gillard became Australia's first female Prime Minister in 2010. On the 21st of March, 2013, Prime Minister Gillard issued a formal apology to all those in Australia who had suffered because of the separations which had occurred through adoption and acknowledged the healing power of an apology, both for those affected and for the nation. The apology included this statement: 'We resolve, as a nation, to do all in our power to make sure these practices are never repeated'. Funds were allocated to provide appropriate services for those affected.

This apology came at the end of a long period in which the understanding and recognition of the long term impact of the separation of children from their families, under a range of circumstances, was gradually brought to the attention of the Australian people. All of these apologies occurred as a result of efforts by many who had suffered the grief and loss associated with separation from family and who had refused to remain silent about their experiences. As a result of their efforts, the people of Australia have been educated, supports and services have been put in place and important lessons have been learned. Australia has set an example to the world.

Adoption and Loss

Part Three

In the 21st Century

Adoption and Loss

Chapter 1 Reflections

In many Western countries, until the early 1970s (and sometimes beyond), there was powerful social support for the practice of removing children from unmarried women and handing them over to married couples. Adoption legislation (which, at that time, was created almost exclusively by men) supported this practice. This occurred in what were essentially male-dominated societies.

In the 1950s, for example, many female teachers in the United Kingdom had to resign from their positions when they married. By the 1960s, they may have been allowed to continue working after marriage, but would commonly be required to resign if they then became pregnant. At this time news of an unmarried woman planning to raise a child alone was often greeted with moral outrage.

In Victorian times, women were not expected to have sexual relationships before they were married, although the same expectations were not generally applied to men. In the nineteenth century, young women were often reaching puberty at the age of fifteen and marrying at the age of seventeen (my great-grandmother married in 1887 at the age of fifteen and gave birth to my grandfather a year later).

By the mid-twentieth century, young women were more likely to reach puberty at the age of twelve and to marry at the age of twenty-two.

Adoption and Loss

Expectations regarding their sexual behaviour, however, did not begin to change until the 1960s. Change was slow and many people at that time were still very critical of unmarried women who became pregnant. Single mothers, more so than single fathers, bore the brunt of society's displeasure. Beliefs about child-rearing were still conservative and the general view was that children raised by one parent instead of two would certainly be disadvantaged. Any woman who expressed the intention to raise a child without a male partner was often accused of being irresponsible.

So entrenched were these attitudes, that it seemed that no one questioned them; they were supported and enacted by women and men alike. Academics and social workers supported them, because they *knew* that allowing children to be raised by a woman alone would result in delinquency. Churches supported them because they *knew* that it was against God's law for women to have children out of wedlock. Politicians supported them with adoption legislation, which ensured that the unmarried mother and her child would not be a drain on the nation's finances. Everyone *knew* that for a single woman with a child, allowing the child to be adopted was 'the right thing to do'. It was considered a wise, unselfish act, a worthy sacrifice in the best interests of the child, a decision for which the young woman could expect a moral pat on the back. My child and I, along with many others, were casualties of this unwritten policy.

Unmarried mothers were viewed at that time, in the society of which I was a part, as a problem. Of course, problems like these are socially constructed. It was not the pregnancy that was a problem, but the circumstances in which the pregnancy existed. That is why all the other new mothers in my maternity ward were being congratulated and showered with gifts when I was not. Their pregnancies existed within socially acceptable parameters. Mine did not. In other times, in other societies, unmarried motherhood was not a problem.

The Hidden Grief

Over time, our society has developed a tolerance for single parenthood and, over time, it seemed that what was once the right thing to do became an awful thing to do. This led women like me to keep it a secret.

When we became pregnant we were made to feel guilty because we had had sex before marriage. When we tried to make amends for that in the way that society dictated, we were made to feel guilty for 'giving away' our children. As time went on, many of us felt, above all else, that we could never find the words to explain our experiences. It was easier not to try.

For many years I did not express the grief that I felt at the loss of my first child. I chose to keep it to myself, because I felt ashamed and embarrassed at what had happened and did not have the confidence to share it with anyone. Now I have accepted my experience and no longer feel apologetic about it. This does not mean that I do not get angry or sad any more. I do. I am angry because I feel that I was taken in. I was duped by a society that told me that my child would be grateful for being 'given away' and that I would get over it because it was for the best. I trusted those who were older and claimed to be wiser.

I am sad that I was persuaded to allow my child to be raised by others. As time went on I realised that I had misjudged the situation. I felt that I had been railroaded by a system that did not recognise my value to my child.

I still have times when I relive the drama of my first pregnancy and the awful emptiness that I felt after my child had been taken from me. I permit myself to experience those feelings when they arise and I accept that they will always be with me. Having been separated from my first child by adoption is an experience that I am reminded of constantly. It is never far from my thoughts, as it affects so many aspects of my life.

When I talk to people about the separation from my son and our reunion, they sometimes ask me why I wanted to 'rake up the past' and why didn't I 'let sleeping dogs lie'. When you give birth to a child, especially when that child still lives, that child does not exist in the past, but in the present. Once you have given birth you are that child's mother and you will always be a mother, no matter what. Being a mother never ends; it is never in the past. Giving birth to a child changes your life forever. You can become an ex-wife, but never an 'ex-mother'.

Many original mothers of adopted children have spent their lives apologising. Some of us apologised for getting pregnant, but many of us were naïve and inexperienced. Some apologised for allowing their babies to be adopted, but many were given no choice, while others were pressured by those in positions of power and control. We were told that we had to put our own feelings to one side and do what we were told would be best for our children. Some have apologised for missing their children and wanting to be reunited with them, but it is a perfectly natural reaction to our loss.

Now that I have explored the events surrounding the loss of my son, I see them as just that, a series of events, without any intrinsic shame or value. It has taken me many years to be able to describe these events, frankly and without apology. Because I have confronted and embraced my experience, I have robbed it of its power to shame and embarrass me.

As I look back over my life, I am reminded that I am responsible for my own choices and for how I respond to the outcomes of those choices. I can now see my trials and tribulations as great opportunities for personal growth. My challenges and sufferings have given me an opportunity to develop both empathy and resilience and, most importantly, to be of service. I am glad that I have lived long enough to understand that my sadness and despair have actually given me a purpose in life – to help others who have suffered through adoption separation and to try to create a kinder future where policies and practices are informed by a genuine consideration for the wellbeing of both vulnerable children and vulnerable parents.

Chapter 2 Consequences

The loss of my first child was the first major loss in my life. The experience was such a painful and complex one that I believe that it has influenced the way that I have responded to subsequent losses. Certain events tap into the pain of that first loss, which, I believe, will always be with me. While I no longer feel shame, that does not mean that I do not suffer. However, I no longer deny my grief and I no longer suppress it.

There have been several major losses in my life since the loss of my son. The first was the loss of my marriage. It hurt me terribly to end my marriage, as being happily married with children was my way of atoning for the 'mistake' of my first child. My self-esteem was very low after the birth of my first son and being able to present the facade of a contented, conventional family was very important to me. It was one way of regaining society's approval. It was difficult to give that up and admit what I, at the time, perceived to be yet another failure. I felt very guilty that my four children might suffer because we were a single parent family.

My first son was born on my brother's birthday. My brother was abroad at the time and when I did see him again, we never talked about my child. After I had told my other four children about Stephen, I decided to talk to my brother and explain to him how it had all come about. I took him out to lunch and recounted my experience to him. It was such a relief to be able to share that with him finally. Three weeks later he was dead, at the age of forty-five, from a brain haemorrhage. I am sorry that he and Stephen were never able to meet, but I am glad that I was able to share my story with him.

After my mother died suddenly and unexpectedly, in 1993, I was in a state of shock. I felt that I had not prepared myself for life without her. I missed her terribly and cried every day for a year. My children adored her and she was like an extra parent to them. Moving to Australia meant that my children were able to spend a lot of time with my mother and I know that they all have many cherished memories of the time that they shared with her. I am very happy that she was able to meet Stephen again before she died. I had no regrets after my mother died. I know that she knew how much I loved and appreciated her and, although her death was very sudden, I felt that there was nothing left undone and nothing left unsaid. Having considered these feelings, I reached the conclusion that I had actually learned from my previous losses and that I had prepared myself for my mother's death without realising I was doing so.

After her death, I found among her special possessions a slip of paper. It took me a long time to identify it, as it had what appeared to be a date on it, but only the day and the month, not the year. Eventually I realised that it was the receipt from the registry office in Edinburgh where we registered Stephen's birth together. I never knew that she had kept it. In twenty-three years, she never mentioned it to me, even after she had met him. My mother taught me many lessons in her life. One stands out. Mum always said, *Children don't owe their parents anything. The child didn't ask to be born.* Mum was right. Children raised by their natural parents don't owe them anything for their efforts. Children raised by adoptive parents do not owe them anything either. Whoever chooses to raise a child, whether their own or someone else's, owes that child the best upbringing they can provide.

The Hidden Grief

I still miss my mother, but she lives on in my children and grandchildren. I believe that they have all inherited a share of her spirit of adventure, her intellectual curiosity, her sense of humour, her generosity and her determination.

When my first grandchild was stillborn, in 1996, I was not only heart-broken, but also very angry. I felt that it was so unfair that I should lose my first child through adoption and then lose my first grandchild also, through death. My first grandchild was one of twin boys. The second twin died shortly after birth. Being a bereaved grandparent, I hurt for the loss of my grandchildren, but I also hurt to see the sufferings of my son and his wife. As a parent, I wanted to heal their pain, but I was very aware of my helplessness. When I knew that I was going to be a grandparent for the first time, I crocheted a large white shawl for the baby; the same type of shawl which I had crocheted for the first child of my marriage, twenty-one years before.

Then I discovered that twins were expected and I hastily crocheted a second white shawl. I was so happy to know that they would not be destroyed the way the first shawl was. My twin grandsons were wrapped together, in the shawls that I had made for them, in their little, white coffin. I was so angry at our loss. I so much wanted the births of all of my grandchildren to be completely happy events, with no tinge of sadness. It was not to be. I will never forget my two little grandsons and, happily, their parents went on to have four more children. Now, in 2018, I have eight surviving grandchildren and I love spending time with them.

After the death of my mother, I cared for my father for four years, until he died in 1997. It was not easy. He missed my mother terribly. I spent those four years working very hard to keep his spirits up. He was not always appreciative. I did it because I had promised my mother that I would make sure that he was looked after if she died before he did. I felt that I owed it to her, if not to him. During the four years that I cared for him, however, he slowly came to appreciate my efforts and achievements. I heard

Adoption and Loss

him say *Thank you* to me for the first time in my life, only after my mother died. I slowly came to understand how much he had lost and what he had missed in his life. We finally learned to make allowances for each other and developed a kind of friendship.

After his death, I was chatting to one of his neighbours and she said, *You know that your Dad was very proud of you?* No, I didn't know that, actually, because, of course, while he may have told others, he refrained from telling me. I believe that his parenting philosophy was never to appear to be impressed by your children's achievements, otherwise they may rest on their laurels. It was a common approach of Scottish parents of his generation.

All of these other losses have drawn me back to that early loss and I have relived it on each occasion. All of these losses are a part of my life. They have helped to shape me and to teach me. I have no doubt that there will be other losses in my life, but I will experience them, I will confront them and I will incorporate them into my life. Never again will I hide, deceive and feel shame. There will be no more secrets and no more lies.

When I was a child, I wanted to travel, gain an education and undertake challenging and fulfilling employment. When I discovered, in October 1969, that I was pregnant, I thought that my plan had been sabotaged.

Like many Scottish children, however, I grew up with the story of King Robert the Bruce, who watched the spider trying to make a web and learned to try, try, try again and never give up trying to defeat the English and maintain Scotland's independent status. I discovered many years later, while researching my family history, that Robert the Bruce, who was King of Scotland from 1306 to 1329, was my 17xgreat-grandfather. Like my ancestor, King Robert, I did not give up.

I have no regrets about the experiences which I have had throughout my life. I have learned many valuable lessons from the risks which I have taken. In my view there are no such things as mistakes in life, only learning opportunities. Like everyone else, I

The Hidden Grief

have had setbacks and disappointments, but I have been able to survive them with my faith in myself intact.

When I consider my journey through life, I believe that I have achieved my goals, not *because* of the fact that my son was adopted, but *in spite* of it.

In fact, I have done all of the things that I wanted to do and I have certainly achieved my goal of having an interesting life. I am grateful to Mr Mackay, my primary school headmaster, for seeing my potential and encouraging my parents to allow me to develop it. I am grateful to my mother for supporting me in pursuing my education. I know that I worked hard to make the most of my opportunities.

I received my Master of Arts degree (an undergraduate degree since the university was founded in the sixteenth century) from the University of Edinburgh in 1970. I then moved to Bermuda, took up a teaching appointment and spent four very happy years working there.

I married, returned to Scotland and had four planned and very much wanted children. I then moved with my children to Australia, a totally unknown country to me. I chose to be a full-time mother for ten years, from the birth of the first child of my marriage, until my youngest child started school.

Within three years of arriving in Australia, I had completed a post-graduate Diploma in Education at the University of Adelaide and started work as a high school teacher. I then returned to study in 1995, completed a post-graduate degree in social work at Flinders University and subsequently was employed as a social worker and counsellor in a range of fields, for seventeen years, before deciding to retire from paid employment in 2013.

Whatever else my life has been, it has never been boring. When I left Renfrew as a seventeen-year-old in 1967 to live in Edinburgh, I felt as if it was the other side of the world. Now I am truly on the other side of the world.

Adoption and Loss

I have spent many years helping those whose lives have been affected by adoption separation. I have presented conference papers and workshops on adoption issues, I have been interviewed by the media on adoption-related topics, I have counselled many people on a one-to-one basis, I have lobbied politicians and I have shared ideas with many people around the world. I have also written and published four books. I now enjoy a busy but relaxed retirement, which includes voluntary work and spending time with my husband and our families.

Chapter 3 What is adoption?

What is adoption? What does it do? Adoption is a legal arrangement by which a child ceases to be the legal child of his or her original/genetic parents and becomes instead the legal child of his or her adoptive parents.

An adopted child is issued with a new birth certificate and the original birth certificate is no longer a legal document (unless an integrated birth certificate is available). This means that (in many parts of the world) the official birth certificates of those who are adopted bear the false information that their adoptive mothers gave birth to them and that they are genetically related to the two people who are their legal parents.

For those who are not adopted, their birth certificate is a document which provides details of their birth, as one would expect, that is, the name of the woman who gave birth to them and where and when this occurred. The birth certificate of an adopted person could state that they were born in a location which their adoptive mother had never actually visited.

This document will be used by the adopted person for all official purposes, for the rest of their life, unless they are able to have their adoption discharged. Generally speaking, the new identity of the child after adoption is not available to any members of the families of origin, at least until the child reaches adulthood and, in many parts of the world, not even then.

221

Adoption and Loss

Adoption permanently severs all legal, family connections between the adopted child and all members of his or her families of origin (ie the family of the mother and the family of the father) including siblings (whether born before or after the adoption), grandparents, cousins and others. In all jurisdictions of which I am aware, once a child is adopted, the original parents have no legal right to any information about that child. For example, they will generally not be told if the adoption has been terminated or if the child has died. In some parts of the world, arrangements are made for what is sometimes called 'open adoption', which can involve regular meetings or sharing of information between the adopted child and their original relatives. However, these are generally not legally enforceable and anecdotal evidence suggests that they are often short-lived.

Any children for whom adoption is being considered are children at risk, because they have found themselves unable to be adequately cared for by the families into which they were born. Removing a child from their family creates a family breakdown. To add to this disadvantage by changing the child's identity is, in my view, immoral. A person who is adopted grows up with the tension created by the pretence of adoption. For example, some adopted people, when questioned by medical professionals, present the medical history of their adoptive parents.

Sometimes this is done because they have absorbed the idea that they are a member of this family and block out the fact that they actually have no genetic connection to their adoptive parents, ancestors or siblings. Sometimes this is done because they are embarrassed to admit that they have no knowledge at all of their parents' medical history. This is clearly an uncomfortable and potentially dangerous situation for society to create for an individual who requires care.

Adoptions began to be regulated by law in many Western countries in the years after the First World War. The intention was to provide homes for children who, for whatever reason, did not have a family situation in which they could be adequately provided for and cared for. Adoptions probably became secret to protect children from the stigma of illegitimacy and perhaps to protect the adoptive parents from the stigma of infertility. The change of name also made it very difficult, if not impossible, for the original mother ever to find her child again.

Adoptions take place mainly in Western countries. In countries where Islam is influential, for example, there are no adoptions. Ancestry and blood-lines are very meaningful and cannot be manipulated and falsified. Children can be cared for by people other than their parents, but the child's identity will not be disguised.

Traditionally, adoption has operated to transfer children from the weak to the powerful and from the poor to the financially secure. While in the past many believed that adoption was a solution to society's problems, we now know that a heavy price has been paid by those involved for what appeared, at the time - to some - to be a simple answer.

Every child is created with a genetic contribution from both a woman and a man. When those genetic connections are denied and omitted from official records, this can cause the child to feel disadvantaged and disconnected. Many people around the world spend a great deal of time and money tracing their ancestors, that is, their blood relatives. For those who have been legally detached from their genetic origins, that process can be extremely difficult and, in some cases, impossible.

In recent years we have become aware of the outcomes for children who were separated from their mothers shortly after birth. During gestation, children become accustomed to their mother's way of moving and to her voice and are born with the expectation that they will remain close to this woman who has given them life. Removing them from their mothers and putting them in the care of different, unknown mothers, can be a traumatic experience, with long-lasting psychological outcomes.

Adoption and Loss

This has relevance not only for adoption, but also in situations of assisted conception, where children are being created using sperm and/or egg donation and 'surrogate' mothers (who often are actually mothers) and then raised by people who have not contributed to their genetic make-up. These arrangements present complex ethical issues.

Children who have been born as a result of such practices, who are now adults, are beginning to make their views known about these processes in the way that adults who were adopted as children have done.

It is my view that, based on what we have learned over the years from the long term outcomes of adoption, the practice of issuing dishonest 'birth certificates', which do not actually represent the details of the child's birth and parentage, but instead indicate the identities of the child's legal guardians, is insupportable and should be discontinued.

For children whose legal parents are not also their genetic parents, then I believe that we have a responsibility to provide them with an honest record of their family relationships. **Acknowledging a birth with a certificate which is blatantly dishonest is an insult to the child.**

Honouring the child's right to the truth about their heritage, an integrated birth certificate would be appropriate, similar to those which are available in South Australia for children who have been adopted. This would provide an honest statement of the child's genetic parentage and the true details of the child's birth, as well as stating the names of the guardians of the child, for practical and legal purposes. Such a document would indicate respect and consideration for the child and acknowledgement of their basic right to know who they are.

In some parts of the world, adults who were adopted as children are still fighting to obtain the truth about their origins. Their justified anger and struggle for access to their heritage should inform practices around assisted conception.

The Hidden Grief

Adoption was designed as a service for children who were perceived to be at a disadvantage in life, not as a service for adults who wanted 'to create a family', which is how many people perceived it by the middle of the twentieth century.

In most jurisdictions, legislation traditionally did not allow for money to change hands as a component of the adoption process. Sadly, however, in some parts of the world, in the twenty-first century, adoption agencies exist to arrange adoptions as a commercial transaction. This commodification of children is repugnant to many in countries such as Australia, where it is illegal.

Happily, much has changed in the (almost) half-century since the birth of my son. No longer are new-born babies routinely torn from the arms of weeping unmarried mothers. The reasons for this dramatic change are fairly obvious. Sexual relationships outside of marriage are now more socially acceptable and contraception and termination are now more readily available. Attitudes to single parenthood have changed considerably over the years and it is evident that there is much more tolerance now for women (or, indeed, men) raising children alone.

A sign of this acceptance is the fact that, in countries, such as Australia, in which government payments are available to parents, they do not distinguish between married and unmarried parents.

Also, the long term impact of adoption separation on people's lives is now much clearer than it was in the past, because those who have spent many years living with the outcomes of adoption separation have been prepared to reveal their experiences publicly. This long term view was not available half a century ago when so many adoptions were taking place.

The outcome of this is that fewer people are willing to become involved in adoptions. This explains the very low number of adoptions of Australian-born children at the moment, in comparison with the numbers fifty years ago.

Adoption and Loss

Thousands of children were adopted in Western countries in the 1960s and 1970s and beyond. Thousands of original mothers and fathers were separated from their children. When I discussed this with one adoptive mother back in 1998 when I first wrote this book, she said that she believed that, one day, we would look back at adoption and wonder how we could have done it. I told her that she didn't have to wait, that people were saying that already.

Sadly, some of those who have experienced adoption separation in their lives feel insulted when adoption is criticised. Criticising adoption is not the same as criticising those who have been involved in adoption. We should all welcome an explanation of the motives behind adoption and an exploration of its outcomes. I am concerned for everyone whose life has been affected by adoption separation. I hope that they will all be prepared to read, to listen, to consider and to learn.

When I first wrote this book twenty years ago, I stated clearly my opinion that we had a moral obligation to replace adoption with more child-centred options. I have been repeating that opinion consistently since that time.

As Joss Shawyer said in 1985:

'Women can and must stop putting in orders for other women's babies'.

Chapter 4 Does adoption have a future?

In Australia the approach to adoption has changed and developed throughout the twentieth century and into the twenty-first and it has been influenced by those whose lives have been affected by adoption separation and who have been prepared to share their experiences and their opinions. Adoption in Australia is under the jurisdiction of the individual governments of each state and territory and privately arranged adoptions are not permitted.

Local adoptions
According to statistics provided by the Australian Institute of Health and Welfare, 9,798 Australian-born children were adopted in Australia in 1972, when the population of Australia was just over 13 million. In 2017, by which time the population had risen to almost 24.5 million, only 246 Australian-born children were adopted. This was the lowest number since records have been kept and represented a 60% decline in the number of adoptions over the previous 25 years. Clearly, we are learning from the mistakes of the past.

Intercountry adoptions
Children have been adopted into Australia from other countries since the 1960s. The annual number of intercountry adoptions peaked at 450 in 1990. Since then, there has been a steady decline

in numbers. This has occurred because many people, in Australia and in other countries, have been speaking out against the practice of removing children from their homelands and extended families to send them to live with strangers in countries whose language and way of life are foreign to them. There is now more support for assisting other countries to care for their children, rather than removing them. In 2017, only 69 children were adopted into Australia from other countries.

Adoption in the 21st century

The principal reason for the reduction in the number of adoptions in Australia is that there is an increased awareness that adoption is not in the best interests of children and we are now developing more appropriate alternatives for children in need of care and protection. Australia is now a leading light in showing the world how to replace adoption with child-centred options.

In the current century, the principal reason for Australian children not being raised by their parents is concern over their safety and well-being. Adoption is not a helpful option for these children and so, for children at risk, permanent guardianship orders are becoming more common. South Australia now has an Other Person Guardianship Policy.

Other Person Guardianship

An Other Person Guardianship order is a legal arrangement whereby vulnerable children who cannot live with their families of origin due to abuse, neglect or parental incapacity cease to be in state care and instead are in the care of one or two people who are appointed as guardians by the Youth Court, after having been assessed for their suitability. Guardians will often be people who are already known to the child eg foster carers or relatives.

Through Other Person Guardianship, these children are provided with **permanent**, stable homes. Those who wish to be guardians must have a willingness to support the child in their care to maintain his or her connection with the family of origin, if it is safe to do so. When a guardianship order is enacted, there is no change of identity; the child retains his or her original birth certificate and remains a member of his or her family of origin.

In South Australia, the number of adoptions of Australian-born children in 1971 was 879. By 1998, that number had dropped to just 4. In the twenty-first century (current population close to 2 million people), the numbers are still very low. In 2010, there were 5, in 2011, 4, in 2012, 1, in 2013, 2, in 2014, 1, and 3 each year in 2015, 2016 and 2017. As the number of children being adopted in South Australia decreases, the number of children being placed under guardianship orders increases. In 2016, 18 children were placed under guardianship orders and in 2017, there were 45.

The future of adoption
In my submission to the Review of the South Australian Adoption Act in 2015, I stated my opinion that: *We have no further need of an Adoption Act to regulate the outcomes for South Australian children who are in need of care, as the Children's Protection Act, 1993, ... covers the needs of children at risk. All children for whom adoption was considered appropriate in the past are now considered to be children at risk and, as such, are catered for under the Children's Protection Act of 1993.*

In line with the findings of the 2014-2015 review of the South Australian Adoption Act, there is now a formal policy in place in South Australia to change the placement arrangements for children who are currently in foster care into permanent guardianship orders.

Although there will always be losses experienced by children who are separated from their families of origin, with guardianship, there is none of the damaging secrecy and pretence which traditionally have been integral elements of adoption. For many years I have been promoting the use of guardianship orders to replace adoption and this is now taking place in Australia. **Between 2011 and 2016, the number of guardianship orders enacted in Australia increased by 84%.**

Role of politicians

In democratic countries, politicians are paid to represent the people who vote for them and to propose and support legislation which is in the best interests of those people. The positive changes which have taken place in Australia in relation to adoption have come about because politicians have listened to those who have experienced the outcomes of family separations which were caused by adoption.

For those in other parts of the world who would like to see similar changes take place in their locations, I suggest that you contact politicians, educate them about the long term impact of adoption and ask them to support changes which will be in the best interests of their communities.

My expectation is, as it has been for the last twenty years, that, in the near future, not only in Australia, but around the world, adoptions will be replaced by more child-centred arrangements such as permanent guardianship orders, which maintain and honour the original family relationships. I hope that the history of change in Australia will inspire those in other countries who would like to see change in their locations. In relation to access to adoption information, government funding for post-adoption support services, apologies and an end to adoption altogether – be assured that **change is possible**.

The Hidden Grief

{This article was first published in the *Australian Journal of Adoption, Vol 2, No 1 (2010).*
© Evelyn Robinson, 2010}

Intercountry adoption - being part of the solution

Domestic adoption in Australia

The history of domestic adoption in Australia is similar to that in most other English-speaking countries, such as New Zealand, Canada and the United Kingdom. In the middle of the twentieth century, single parenthood was socially shameful for both parents and children. Vulnerable parents (usually unmarried mothers) were not considered to be competent enough to raise their children, who were transferred to the care of supposedly more competent parents (usually childless, infertile and relatively affluent couples), who had society's approval, because they were married.

Unsupported mothers were rendered powerless owing to the shame and blame inflicted on them by the rigid social expectations of the times. Government financial support was practically non-existent, as was childcare. Adoption was encouraged as being in the best interests of everyone, especially the children. Adoption was about ***affluence vs poverty, competence vs incompetence and power vs powerlessness***.

Intercountry adoption in Australia

After the Sole Parent Pension was introduced in Australia by the Federal Government in 1973, numbers of adoptions of Australian born children reduced dramatically. In social welfare terms, this was seen as a positive change. However, it soon became obvious that there was a noticeable increase in the number of children being adopted into Australia from other countries. This suggests that intercountry adoption grew to meet an increasing demand for children on behalf of those who wished to adopt.

According to the Hague Convention, intercountry adoption is supposed to be about providing care for children in need. There are, of course, needy children in almost every country in the world. However, children are adopted between poverty-stricken countries and affluent countries, almost exclusively in one direction. On a global scale, it appears that intercountry adoption, in the twenty-first century, is still about *affluence vs poverty, competence vs incompetence and power vs powerlessness*.

Affluence, competence and power

Affluent countries have had the resources and the time to develop the competence to care for children and families in need and to alleviate poverty, to a much greater degree than the countries which are generally described as 'third world'. Countries which are affluent and are considered to be competent are powerful in the global community. Many view intercountry adoption as a hangover from the patronising days of colonialism, which has prevented struggling economies from developing their own internal social welfare programmes, by perpetuating a culture of dependence and helplessness.

Intercountry adoption does not reduce poverty in third world countries, nor increase their confidence in their ability to care for their needy children. Instead of strengthening those countries by sharing our affluence, competence and power with them, we are removing their precious resources (their children), which weakens their communities and allows us to bask in our feelings of superiority and benevolence.

The Hidden Grief

Through intercountry adoption, children are being removed from their family, their language, their culture, their community, their homeland and their heritage and scattered throughout the world. This causes pain and suffering to those communities and countries, who are losing their future generations, not to mention the loss and grief experienced by the children themselves. The lifelong issues for those children are of enormous concern, which will not be addressed here.

Australia gained the admiration and respect of the world by apologising to our Aboriginal people for the removal of children which led to the tragedies of the Stolen Generations. However, our international reputation is now being tarnished, as we are using our affluence, competence and power to exploit third world countries, by removing their children from them. Our government may one day be delivering an apology to the children who have been adopted into Australia from other countries.

Issues for children around the world

Poverty is the greatest single problem affecting children in the world today. Hungry children need food. Sick children need medicine. They do not need adoption. Australia and other affluent countries are in a position to provide social aid to countries struggling with poverty, to support families and communities in need and to provide them with training and expertise to set up government and community-based programmes to provide long term assistance. In this way other countries will be empowered to care for their needy families who encounter poverty and disaster in ways that are culturally appropriate and respectful, instead of having their families and communities fractured.

In some countries adoptions take place, not because of poverty, but because pregnancies occur in socially unacceptable situations. Social attitudes in Australia and other English-speaking countries have changed enormously in the last half-century and they are beginning to change in other countries. Australia can assist in the process of change and cease to collude in supporting conditions of social inequality, by removing these 'inconvenient' children.

Being part of the solution

Australians have for many years contributed to ethical programmes, which support many countries to develop social supports for communities, families and individuals in need. Those who contribute have the satisfaction of knowing that they have helped to educate and empower, to preserve cultural traditions, to encourage equity and dignity and to keep families together. Our government can build on the good work that is being done already and thereby enhance Australia's international reputation. The time has come for Australia to take a stand and set an example to other 'first world' nations. There are many Australians who would like to see immediate plans put in place by Australia to end intercountry adoption. Let us share our *affluence, competence* and *power* for the benefit of children in need around the world. Many Australians would be proud to see Australia become part of the solution, instead of continuing to contribute to the problem.

~~~~~~~~~~~~~~~~~~~~~~~~~~~~~~~~~~~~

The Hidden Grief

Bibliography

Berryman, Sarah, *Understanding Reunion: Reflections on Research from the Post-Adoption Resource Centre, NSW,* in Separation, Reunion, Reconciliation, Proceedings from the Sixth Australian Conference on Adoption, Brisbane, 1997

Dessaix, Robert, *A Mother's Disgrace*, HarperCollins, Sydney, 1994

Doka, Kenneth, *Disenfranchised Grief: Recognizing Hidden Sorrow*, Lexington Books, Lexington, MA., 1989

Hale, Meg, *Mothers in ARMS*, Wakefield Press, South Australia, 2014

Inglis, Kate, *The Relinquishment Process and Grieving*, Third Australian Conference on Adoption, Adelaide, 1982.

Inglis, K., *Living Mistakes - Mothers who consented to adoption*, Allen & Unwin, Sydney, 1984

Kauffman, Jeffrey, *Intrapsychic Dimensions of Disenfranchised Grief*, Chapter 3 in Disenfranchised Grief, edited by Kenneth Doka, Lexington Books, Lexington, MA., 1989

Kuhn, Dale, *A Pastoral Counselor Looks at Silence as a Factor in Disenfranchised Grief*, Chapter 21 in Disenfranchised Grief, edited by Kenneth Doka, Lexington Books, Lexington, MA., 1989

Lennon, Ingrid Pedersen, *Mon frère s'appelait John Lennon* (*My brother's name was John Lennon*), Michel Lafon, 2005.

Lifton, Betty Jean, *Journey of the Adopted Self*, Basic Books, 1994.

Meagher, David, *The Counselor and the Disenfranchised Griever*, Chapter 27 in Disenfranchised Grief, edited by Kenneth Doka, Lexington Books, Lexington, MA., 1989

Nichols, Jane, *Perinatal Loss*, Chapter 11 in Disenfranchised Grief, edited by Kenneth Doka, Lexington Books, Lexington, MA, 1989.

Pavao, Dr Joyce Maguire, *Healing Stories*, in Adoption and Healing, Proceedings of the international conference on Adoption and Healing, New Zealand Adoption Education and Healing Trust, 1997

Pine, Vanderlyn, *Death, Loss, and Disenfranchised Grief*, Chapter 2 in Disenfranchised Grief, edited by Kenneth Doka, Lexington Books, Lexington, MA., 1989

Shawyer, Joss, *Death by Adoption*, Cicada Press, New Zealand, 1979

Shawyer, Joss, *The Politics of Adoption*, Healthright, Vol.5, No.1, November 1985.

Silverman, Phyllis, *Helping Women Cope with Grief*, Sage Publications, California, 1981

Small, Joanne, *Working with Adoptive Families*, Public Welfare, Summer 1987

van Keppel, M., Midford, S. & Cicchini, M, *The Experience of Loss in Adoption*, Fifth National Conference, National Association for Loss and Grief, Perth, September, 1987.

Verrier, Nancy, *The Primal Wound: Legacy of Adoption*, presented at the American Congress International Convention, California, USA, April, 1991

Verrier, Nancy, *The Primal Wound*, Gateway Press, Baltimore, USA, 1993

Verrier, Nancy, *Separation Trauma*, in Separation, Reunion, Reconciliation, Proceedings from the Sixth Australian Conference on Adoption, Brisbane, 1997

Winkler, R. & van Keppel, M., *The Effect on the Mother of Relinquishing a Child for Adoption*, Third Australian Conference on Adoption, Adelaide, 1982.

Winkler, R., van Keppel, M., *Relinquishing Mothers in Adoption, Their long-term adjustment,* Melbourne Institute of Family Studies, Monograph no.3, 1984

Worden J. W., *Grief Counselling & Grief Therapy*, Tavistock/Routledge, London, 1982

National Apology for Forced Adoptions
21 March 2013

1. Today, this Parliament, on behalf of the Australian people, takes responsibility and apologises for the policies and practices that forced the separation of mothers from their babies, which created a lifelong legacy of pain and suffering.

2. We acknowledge the profound effects of these policies and practices on fathers.

3. And we recognise the hurt these actions caused to brothers and sisters, grandparents, partners and extended family members.

4. We deplore the shameful practices that denied you, the mothers, your fundamental rights and responsibilities to love and care for your children. You were not legally or socially acknowledged as their mothers. And you were yourselves deprived of care and support.

5. To you, the mothers who were betrayed by a system that gave you no choice and subjected you to manipulation, mistreatment and malpractice, we apologise.

6. We say sorry to you, the mothers who were denied knowledge of your rights, which meant you could not provide informed consent. You were given false assurances. You were forced to endure the coercion and brutality of practices that were unethical, dishonest and in many cases illegal.

7. We know you have suffered enduring effects from these practices forced upon you by others. For the loss, the grief, the disempowerment, the stigmatisation and the guilt, we say sorry.

8. To each of you who were adopted or removed, who were led to believe your mother had rejected you and who were denied the opportunity to grow up with your family and community of origin and to connect with your culture, we say sorry.

9. We apologise to the sons and daughters who grew up not knowing how much you were wanted and loved.

10. We acknowledge that many of you still experience a constant struggle with identity, uncertainty and loss, and feel a persistent tension between loyalty to one family and yearning for another.

11. To you, the fathers, who were excluded from the lives of your children and deprived of the dignity of recognition on your children's birth records, we say sorry. We acknowledge your loss and grief.

12. We recognise that the consequences of forced adoption practices continue to resonate through many, many lives. To you, the siblings, grandparents, partners and other family members who have shared in the pain and suffering of your loved ones or who were unable to share their lives, we say sorry.

13. Many are still grieving. Some families will be lost to one another forever. To those of you who face the difficulties of reconnecting with family and establishing ongoing relationships, we say sorry.

14. We offer this apology in the hope that it will assist your healing and in order to shine a light on a dark period of our nation's history.

15. To those who have fought for the truth to be heard, we hear you now. We acknowledge that many of you have suffered in silence for far too long.

16. We are saddened that many others are no longer here to share this moment. In particular, we remember those affected by these practices who took their own lives. Our profound sympathies go to their families.

17. To redress the shameful mistakes of the past, we are committed to ensuring that all those affected get the help they need, including access to specialist counselling services and support, the ability to find the truth in freely available records and assistance in reconnecting with lost family.

18. We resolve, as a nation, to do all in our power to make sure these practices are never repeated. In facing future challenges, we will remember the lessons of family separation. Our focus will be on protecting the fundamental rights of children and on the importance of the child's right to know and be cared for by his or her parents.

19. With profound sadness and remorse, we offer you all our unreserved apology.

**Delivered by the Prime Minister of Australia,
The Honourable Julia Gillard**

Adoption and Loss

About the Author

Evelyn Robinson, OAM is an internationally acclaimed author, consultant and educator, who speaks and writes from both a personal and a professional perspective about adoption separation and its long term outcomes. Evelyn is an unaffiliated adoption activist and advocate, based in South Australia, who has contributed in many ways for many years to educating the community about the long term outcomes of adoption separation and assisting family members who have experienced it. Evelyn has also consistently promoted guardianship as a more child-centred alternative to adoption. Evelyn has never charged a fee for any of her speaking engagements or training sessions, although she has, on occasion, accepted payment which was offered.

1949: Evelyn was born in Renfrew, Scotland.

1970: Evelyn graduated from the University of Edinburgh, Scotland with a Master of Arts degree. Evelyn also gave birth to her first child, Stephen, who was subsequently adopted into another family.

1970-1974: Evelyn moved to Bermuda, taught at the Berkeley Institute and married her first husband.

1974 – 1982: Evelyn returned to live in Renfrew, gave birth to four children and then divorced her first husband.

1982: Evelyn moved to South Australia with her children.

1984: Evelyn completed a Post Graduate Certificate in Education at the University of Adelaide, South Australia.

Adoption and Loss

1989: Evelyn joined ARMS in South Australia and was a Management Committee member and Newsletter Editor between 1993 and 1999. Evelyn was a member of ARMS until 2004.

1991: Evelyn and Stephen were reunited when Stephen visited Australia for the first time.

1996: Evelyn completed a Bachelor of Social Work degree at Flinders University, South Australia.

1997: On the 8th of June, 1997, a letter to the editor written by Evelyn was published in the *Sunday Mail* (South Australia) newspaper. In this letter, Evelyn raised the possibility of a federal apology for past adoption policies and practices. This is believed to be the first public reference to the possibility of a National Adoption Apology in Australia.

Evelyn provided a training session in the long term implications of adoption separation for students at the Adelaide College of Divinity, South Australia, as part of the *Diploma in Ministry* course.

1998: Evelyn presented a training session for social workers employed by Centrelink (now part of the Australian Government Department of Human Services) in South Australia on disenfranchised grief with an emphasis on its relevance for adoption.

Evelyn provided a training session in adoption separation and reunion experiences for staff at the South Australian Department of Human Services in the *Adoption and Family Information Service*, in South Australia.

1999: Evelyn commenced employment with ARMS in South Australia as their Counsellor/Co-ordinator.

The Hidden Grief

Evelyn provided a training session for staff at OARS (Offenders Aid and Rehabilitation Services of SA Inc) in South Australia on loss and grief issues in relation to adoption separation and reunion.

2000: Evelyn published her first book, **Adoption and Loss – *The Hidden Grief.***
	Evelyn also presented a training session for the University of Adelaide, South Australia, to students enrolled in the *Graduate Certificate in Bereavement and Palliative Care.* The session was entitled *Losses relating to adoption and separation from children.*

2001: In March, Evelyn presented two seminars in Western Australia for ARCS (Adoption Research and Counselling Service Inc) and a seminar for the University of Western Australia. Evelyn was also guest speaker at the AGM of ARMS (Association Representing Mothers Separated from their children by adoption) in Western Australia.
	Beginning in April 2001, Evelyn travelled for three months, in her own time and at her own expense, to New Zealand, the USA, Canada, England, Scotland, the Republic of Ireland and Northern Ireland and presented on twenty-one occasions for various organisations. This included presenting a paper at the American Adoption Congress conference in Anaheim, California. Some of these presentations were arranged for a professional audience and others for members of the public.

2002: Evelyn supervised a final year social work student while working as a post-adoption counsellor at ARMS in South Australia.

2003: Evelyn resigned from her position as Counsellor/Co-ordinator with ARMS in South Australia.
Evelyn presented at the CUB (Concerned United Birthparents) Retreat in Virginia, USA.

Adoption and Loss

2004: Evelyn published her second book, **Adoption and Recovery - *Solving the Mystery of Reunion*** while working privately as a post adoption counsellor, with local and international clients.

Evelyn travelled in her own time and at her own expense to New Zealand where she presented on ten occasions in Christchurch, Dunedin, Wellington, Auckland and Rotorua. Separate presentations were arranged in each location for members of the public and for interested professionals. On her way to New Zealand, Evelyn also addressed members of a support group called ALAS (Adoption Loss Adult Support Australia Inc) in Queensland.

In September, Evelyn was guest speaker at the VANISH (Victorian Adoption Network for Information and Self-Help) AGM in Melbourne, Australia.

2005: In April Evelyn presented two seminars in Sydney, Australia for PARC (Post Adoption Resource Centre).

In July Evelyn presented two seminars in Melbourne, Australia with her son, Stephen, for VANISH. Evelyn also addressed a support group of members of ARMS Victoria.

In June Evelyn was interviewed by the British Broadcasting Corporation (BBC) for a programme called *Woman's Hour.* When the programme was broadcast, they described her as '*renowned internationally as a leading authority on the subject*' (of the long term outcomes of adoption separation).

In September and October Evelyn travelled for five weeks, in her own time and at her own expense, and spoke in Ireland (Dublin and Cork), Scotland (Edinburgh and Renfrew), Canada (Toronto) and in the USA at the CUB (Concerned United Birthparents) Retreat (Pacific Grove, California). Her visit to Scotland included being guest speaker at the 21st Anniversary of the Adoption Contact Register for Scotland, an event which was organised by the staff of Birthlink, who manage the register. Evelyn was also guest speaker at the morning assembly at Paisley Grammar

244

School, where she was a pupil from 1961 - 1967. Evelyn received a warm welcome from the Rector and pupils and donated copies of her books to the school library.

2006: In October Evelyn presented a seminar with her son, Stephen, in Adelaide, South Australia for the newly-formed, government funded Post Adoption Support Service (PASS).

2007: Evelyn provided a training session on the long term outcomes of adoption separation for Lifeline (a twenty-four hour crisis and referral line) staff in South Australia. Evelyn married her second husband (to whom she is still married).

2009: Evelyn published her third book, **Adoption Reunion – Ecstasy or Agony?**
In September 2009, Evelyn's knowledge and expertise were acknowledged by the Australian government and a special position was created for her on the National Intercountry Adoption Advisory Group (NICAAG). This group met on a regular basis to provide advice to the Australian Attorney-General. Evelyn was a member of NICAAG until March, 2012. She is the only mother who has lost a child to adoption to have been appointed to NICAAG, which ceased to exist in 2013.
In November, 2009, Evelyn presented at an adoption forum in Canberra, Australia, to celebrate the tenth anniversary of the founding of the support group Adoption Mosaic. While in Canberra, Evelyn was also present in the Great Hall at New Parliament House for the government's apology to the Forgotten Australians and the Child Migrants.

2010: Evelyn published her fourth book, **Adoption Separation – Then and now.**

Adoption and Loss

In May, Evelyn contributed to the Monash University History of Adoption Project. Evelyn also submitted a copy of *Adoption Separation - Then and now.*

In the Western Australian Parliament, on the 19th of October, 2010, an apology was delivered to those who had been adversely affected by past adoption policies and practices. **This was the first time in the world that a government apologised for adoptions.** Evelyn was present for this important event and was accompanied by her son, Stephen.

After the apology in Western Australia, the Movement for an Adoption Apology (MAA) was formed in the United Kingdom and Evelyn accepted their invitation to be their Honorary Consultant.

2011: In October, 2011, Evelyn was invited to give evidence to the Australian Senate Enquiry into the Commonwealth Contribution to Former Forced Adoption Policies and Practices. Evelyn also submitted a copy of *Adoption Separation - Then and now.*

2012: In February, 2012, Evelyn was invited to contribute to the National Research Study on the Service Response to Past Adoption Experiences conducted by the Australian Institute of Family Studies. Evelyn also submitted a copy of *Adoption Separation - Then and now.*

On the 29th of March, 2012, the South Australian government announced that they would make a formal apology to those whose lives had been adversely affected by past adoption policies and practices. The apology took place on the 18th of July, 2012 at 11.00 am. Evelyn was present for the apology and was accompanied by her husband, Neil, her daughter, Lisa and her son, Stephen. Evelyn had represented the community as a member of the adoption apology working group, which advised the Premier and the Minister responsible for adoptions. The Premier, Jay Weatherill, publicly acknowledged Evelyn's contribution.

The Hidden Grief

In June, 2012, Evelyn was interviewed by Tricia Fronek for 'podsocs', which is a web site of podcasts for social workers.

2013: In the lead-up to the National Apology for Forced Adoptions, Evelyn and her son, Stephen, were interviewed by the Australian Broadcasting Corporation (ABC) for a current affairs programme called *The 7.30 Report.* The programme was broadcast on Friday, 15th March, 2013. The segment was entitled: 'Women who fought for adoption rights'.

On the 21st of March, 2013, at Parliament House, in Canberra, the Australian Prime Minister, Julia Gillard, issued a formal apology to all those in Australia whose lives had been adversely affected by past adoption policies and practices. Evelyn was consulted by the Federal Government and assisted them in formulating the apology. She is proud to have been able to assist in converting the private pain of mothers who have been separated from their children by adoption into a very public issue. Evelyn attended the apology with her son, Stephen, as invited guests of the Attorney-General's Department.

Evelyn was appointed to the Forced Adoptions Implementation Working Group, which was a panel of experts who advised the Federal Government on the implementation of the commitments made at the time of the National Apology for Forced Adoptions. The group met regularly from July, 2013 until December, 2014.

Evelyn was also invited to be a member of an expert group to assist Vanish, in Victoria, Australia, to develop a training programme to increase awareness of adoption issues among professionals. Interviews with Evelyn were included as part of the training materials.

2014: In March, 2014, along with other members of the Forced Adoptions Implementation Working Group, Evelyn was invited to be present in the House of Representatives and in the Senate, at

Adoption and Loss

Parliament House in Canberra, when speeches were made in reference to the first anniversary of the National Apology for Forced Adoptions. Evelyn was also present at the unveiling of the Apology Parchment which will be on permanent display in Parliament House.

2015: In January, Evelyn contributed a submission to the review of the South Australian Adoption Act, which called on the South Australian government to phase out adoptions completely and replace them with Guardianship Orders,

In March, Evelyn was present as an invited guest at the launch of the Forced Adoptions History Project at the National Archives in Canberra.

Evelyn also attended a meeting at the invitation of the Australian Psychological Society to assist them in preparing their training module on post-adoption loss and grief. Evelyn donated copies of her books.

In April, Evelyn was one of the presenters of a training session in Canberra for staff who would be working on the new National Intercountry Adoption Helpline.

2017: Evelyn was named in the Australia Day Honours List and was awarded an Order of Australia Medal (OAM) for her service to the community and in particular to family members separated by adoption. Evelyn attended the award ceremony with her husband, Neil, her son, Winston and her daughter, Lisa.

2018: The South Australian government announced that following the recommendations of the Review of the Adoption Act in 2015, their policy is now to move children in foster care to guardianship relationships.

The Hidden Grief

Publications

1995: Conference paper: <u>Unmasking the Grief of Relinquishing Mothers</u>, (co-presenter), *Unmasking Grief,* National Association for Loss and Grief, 9th Biennial National Conference, September, 1995, Adelaide, South Australia.

Conference paper: <u>Understanding the Loss of a Relinquishing Mother</u> (co-presenter), *Understanding Loss and Managing Change,* National Multidisciplinary Conference, March, 1995, Adelaide, South Australia.

1997: Conference paper: <u>Grief Associated with the Loss of Children to Adoption</u>, *Sixth Australian Conference on Adoption,* Brisbane, Queensland, Australia.

Conference paper: <u>What Does Reconciliation Mean for Original mothers</u>, (co-presenter), *Sixth Australian Conference on Adoption,* Brisbane, Queensland, Australia.

Poster on <u>Adoption and Suicide</u> at the 19th Congress of the International Association for Suicide Prevention, Adelaide.

1997 – 2001: Evelyn was a guest lecturer on several occasions at Flinders University in South Australia, presenting a workshop entitled *Grief Associated with the Loss of a Child through Adoption* to social work students. In 2002, Evelyn's workshop was made available as part of the Flinders University on-line social work degree programme.

1998: Conference paper: <u>Disenfranchised grief: recognising and meeting the needs of parents who have lost children to adoption</u>, *British Association of Social Workers' Seminar,* August, Edinburgh, Scotland.

Conference paper: <u>Post-Relinquishment Grief Counselling</u>, *2nd International Conference on Social Work in Health and Mental Health,* January, Melbourne, Victoria, Australia.

Adoption and Loss

2000: Book: **Adoption and Loss – *The Hidden Grief.***
Conference paper: <u>Mistreated, Mateless Mothers?</u> - The grief experienced by women who have lost children through adoption and the services provided for them, *Seventh Australian Adoption Conference*, Hobart, Tasmania, Australia.

2001: Conference paper: <u>Adoption and Loss - The Hidden Grief</u> - *23rd Annual American Adoption Congress Conference*, April, Anaheim, California, USA.

2002: Journal article: <u>Post Adoption Grief Counselling</u>, *Adoption and Fostering*, the journal of the British Association for Adoption and Fostering (BAAF) Volume 26, Number 2, Summer, 2002. Unfortunately some unauthorised alterations were made to the article and an apology was issued in the following edition of *Adoption and Fostering*.
Evelyn contributed a chapter to a book entitled <u>Adoption: Opposing Viewpoints</u> edited by Roman Espejo and published by Greenhaven Press, San Diego, California.

2003: Book: Revised edition of **Adoption and Loss – *The Hidden Grief.***

2004: Book: **Adoption and Recovery – *Solving the mystery of reunion.***

2006: Conference paper: <u>Adoption Loss and Recovery</u>. Evelyn was keynote speaker in February at an international conference entitled *The Rights of the Child*, in Bucharest, Romania.

The Hidden Grief

2007: Journal article: <u>Long term outcomes of losing a child through adoption: The impact of disenfranchised grief</u>, *Grief Matters*, The Australian Journal of Grief and Bereavement, Autumn 2007 (Volume 10, number 1).

Evelyn provided the foreword for 'The Stork Market *America's Multi-Billion Dollar Unregulated Adoption Industry'*, by Mirah Riben.

2008: Conference paper: <u>Disenfranchised Grief and Adoption Separation</u> - *The 8th International Conference on Grief and Bereavement in Contemporary Society,* July, 2008, Melbourne, Australia.

2009: Book: **Adoption Reunion – *Ecstasy or Agony?***

Journal article: <u>This Wheel's on Fire – How I got fired up about adoption,</u> *Australian Journal of Adoption*, Vol 1, No.2

2010: Book: **Adoption Separation – *Then and now.***

Journal article: <u>Intercountry Adoption – Being part of the solution,</u> *Australian Journal of Adoption*, Vol 2, No.1

Conference paper: <u>Are we creating another stolen generation?</u> - *Interdisciplinary Perspectives on Intercountry Adoption in Australia: History, Policy, Practices and Experience Symposium* at Monash University in Victoria, Australia.

Journal article: <u>Review: Without a Map [a memoir] by Meredith Hall,</u> *Australian Journal of Adoption*, Vol 2, No.1

Journal article: Review: Outsiders Within – Writing on Transracial Adoption, edited by Jane Jeong Trenka, Julia Chinyere Oparah and Sun Yung Shin, *Australian Journal of Adoption*, Vol 2, No.2

Journal article: <u>The Times They Are A'Changin',</u> *Australian Journal of Adoption*, Vol 2, No.3

Adoption and Loss

2011: Conference paper: <u>Adoption in Australia</u>: Evelyn presented a paper at an international conference entitled *Unwed Mothers, Adoption and Gender Law,* at Ewha Womans University in Seoul, South Korea.

2012: Journal article: <u>Apology in South Australia for past adoption policies and practices/One small (apologetic) step for a woman, one giant leap for womankind,</u> *Australian Journal of Adoption,* Vol 4, No.1

Journal article: <u>My Journey of Healing and Understanding - This Wheel's on Fire – How I got fired up about adoption,</u> *Australian Journal of Adoption,* Vol 5, No.2

Conference paper: <u>Sinking the Mother Ship</u>, 10th Australian Adoption Conference, Melbourne, Australia. Published in the *Australian Journal of Adoption,* Vol 6, No.1

2018: Evelyn published this **21ˢᵗ century** edition of her first book, **Adoption and Loss – *The Hidden Grief.***

.

Printed in Great Britain
by Amazon